# The Polish
# TATRA
## an illustrated guide

# The Polish
# TATRA
## an illustrated
## guide

Kurier Geograficzny

**Text and photographs:** Jerzy Kosim
**Editor:** Irena Łopyta
**Translation:** Grzegorz Hołdys
**Cartography:**
© Zakład Kartograficzny Sygnatura
© Wydawnictwo Kartograficzne Polkart
The map of Tatra National Park in 1:25000 scale
**Published by:**
Kurier Geograficzny
ul. Budczycka 15
55-106 Zawonia (Poland)
tel./fax: (48-071) 312 81 58

ISBN 83-913661-1-1

### A word from the translator

When reading the Polish version of this guide I tried to imagine an English-speaking foreigner attempting to pronounce a term like „Mięguszowieckie Szczyty". With this image in mind, driven by the pledge to spare You the pain and suffering of the ultimate tongue-twisters, I decided to translate at least some of the Polish landmark names into English. You will find the translated names in parentheses right after their Polish counterparts. Beware, these are not official translations, you will not find them on any maps, or in any other guides. They may, however, give you a taste of the specific language of the Tatra mountains. The original names of summits, valleys and other landmarks are often descriptive and have an emotional undertone. The unique charm is enhanced by their metaphoric character. The translations appear whenever a new name is introduced, providing that the name can be translated, and then reappear a couple of times in the text.

# Contens:

**Zakopane** is a great place for summer and winter holidays. Its splendid location at the foot of the Tatra mountains makes it an ideal starting point for hiking. The town itself is also a significant tourist attraction. Zakopane was created as a settlement sometime in the XVIth century. Its name appeared for the first time in the XVIIth century. The climatic and tourist virtues of Zakopane were discovered in mid XIXth century. They were vividly advertised among the people of science and art by Tytus Chałubiński (1820-1889). In 1884 a railroad track from Cracow to Chabówka was built. Two years later the town was awarded the status of a health resort. These two events triggered off a steady rise of Zakopane's popularity and hence an equally dynamic growth of the town itself. Many new hotels were created while tourism and winter sport activities flourished.

The reputation of Zakopane as a sport and tourist centre was strengthened in the period between the World Wars. Many prominent writers, painters, scientists and politicians visited the town in that time. The most memorable of them was Stanisław Ignacy Witkiewicz. Many famous people looked for inspiration in Zakopane and its surroundings. Among them were Henryk Sienkiewicz, Ignacy Jan Paderewski, Karol Szymanowski, Jan Kasprowicz, Józef Ignacy Kraszewski. The rapid urbanisation and the introduction of motor vehicles led to the loss of health resort status by Zakopane. In the recent years many attempts were made to salvage the environment and to restore it to its former shape.

Zakopane is a special place not only because of its geographical location or climatic values. Its uniqueness comes from its character, the charm of various places, the language, and most of all, the people who live here. The tourist values of Tatra mountains, with their 300 km of marked foot-paths, of different difficulty levels, are undeniable. Yet it is the folklore that makes this place so special. It is present everywhere, at all times. Clothes,

*Jan Krzeptowski Sabała (1809-1894) – the legend of the Tatra mountains. A highlander musician and story-teller. His monument (sculpted by Jan Nalborczyk) along with the bust of T. Chałubiński stands by the junction of Zamoyskiego and Chałubińskiego Streets.*

6

music, rituals, language, art, craft and architecture make this part of Poland exceptionally attractive and bring about some unforgettable memories. Regional festivities, unique music dance, and original cuisine add to the list of Zakopane's assets.

While visiting Podhale and Zakopane one ought to take note of the local architecture and houses' structure, though the original beauty of buildings will most likely draw one's attention instantly. Sacral structures, as well as houses, pensions and farm buildings are captivating and rich in ornaments. During a period after 1945 the image of Zakopane and its surroundings was distorted by new box-like buildings, which did not match the local traditional architecture. Fortunately this period has ended. Now, all new houses have the typical shape, with its characteristic tall, sloped roof, covered with shingles, or recently, due to economic reasons, with tin. The buildings are made of larch or spruce wood. The type of architecture currently present in Zakopane was developed by Stanisław Witkiewicz and is known as Zakopiański Style. It is most visible in large villas and pensions, build on tall granite foundation with spacious, open porches.

## KRUPÓWKI

Krupówki is the most lively place in Zakopane. This one-kilometre long promenade is probably the most well known street in Poland. Some people like this place, others tend to think of it as a vanity-fair, or a strange Skansen museum. Nevertheless, the street has a specific charm and it clearly portrays the dynamic development of Zakopane through many decades. Could the inconsistency of architecture in this street be a drawback to anyone? Taking a couple of walks down Krupówki on sunny and rainy days, in the morning and in the dusk, looking at the buildings above the shops and the crowd, peeking into the back-yards, should allow you to discover the hidden distinctiveness of this place. The

*Rondo Kuźnickie. Arriving from the centre of Zakopane: Kuźnice – ahead, to the left – Jaszczurówka and the road to Morskie Oko, to the right – ski-jumps • A ski-way on Nosal • A genuine ram shashlik on Gubałówka.*

Zakopane center

9

street is a starting location of numerous foot-paths leading around Zakopane and its neighbourhood. These paths require no special equipment or clothes. A pair of sturdy, comfortable shoes will do. You can take a nice walk, starting at the intersection of Krupówki with Nowotarska and Kościeliska Streets and heading along the Foluszowy stream.

The Church of the Holy Family was completed in 1896 after 19 years of construction work. It was designed by Józef Dziekoński. The main altar, in the form of a triptych, was created in 1903. Side altars and the chapel of Saint Jesus' Heart were designed by Edgar Kováts. The chapel of Virgin Mary's Rosary and John the Baptist's was created by Stanisław Witkiewicz, who also designed the entrance doors, benches, confessionals and bars. Numerous sculptures were created by Jan Nalborczyk.

On the opposite side of the street (after crossing the bridge over the Foluszowy Stream) one can find the Tatra Museum of Dr Tytus Chałubiński. The building was built between 1913 and 1922, according to the projects of Stanisław Witkiewicz and Franciszek Mączyński. The rooms on the ground floor house ethnographic artefacts. Among them is the permanent exposition of highlander's hut and the XIXth century folk art. Local animal and plant life-forms can be seen on the first floor, along with geological collections. The oldest technical school in Zakopane stands beside the museum. It was built in 1883 and currently is known as Władysław Matlakowski's Complex of Technical Schools. Another magnificent structure, the Tatra railroad station built in 1903, stands in the vicinity of the two buildings mentioned earlier.

Making our way back to Krupówki, we pass a horse-carriage stop. On the intersection of Kościuszki and Zaruski Streets, on the right hand side we can see the post office from the beginning of XXth century.

*Highlander wedding in the new st. Cross's Church on Zamoyskiego Street • A row of wooden sculptures on Równia Krupowa (Krupowa Plane).*

Above, stands one of the most significant buildings in Zakopane – the „Morskie Oko" hotel. This one has been standing here since 1901 and was built on the ruins of an earlier, similar construction, that burned down. The hotel is a legend as some of the most famous musicians, politicians and artists stayed here. The celebrities who performed on the special stage in the ball-room include Helena Modrzejewska, Ludwik Solski, Hanka Ordonówna and many more. „Morskie Oko" was especially popular during the twenty years between World Wars.

Further on, heading towards Zamoyski Street, we pass many interesting buildings. Among them a hotel – „Kasprowy Wierch", „Poraj" Restaurant" (1887) and a villa called „Zośka" (around 1900).

## KOŚCIELISKA STREET – THE OLDEST PART OF THE TOWN

Kościeliska Street, stretching from Krupówki to Skibówki, is the oldest street in Zakopane. The original, wooden buildings along it are in a very good condition. The old houses and farmyards owned in the past by rich highlander families, were built somewhere in the XIXth century. They occupy both sides of the street. The old town centre was located around a wooden church, built in 1847, now called the „Old Church". The shops, school, marketplace and pub were all created in that time.

The oldest sacral building of Zakopane is the small chapel, built around 1800, by Paweł Gąsienica. The interior is a modern design by Antoni Kenar, brought to life by Józef Kandefer. Besides the chapel stands a small wooden church constructed by Sebastian Gąsienica Sobczak. It is called the church of Virgin Mary from Częstochowa and Saint Clement. The building was enlarged in 1851 by a parish-priest named Józef Stolarczyk. The church is decorated with XIXth century folk paintings and sculptures.

*Markets of folk art and presentations of traditional methods of art-making, organised during the annual International Festival of the Folklore of Mountain Regions in August.*

**Krupówki.** The main street of Zakopane. It probably owes its name to a nearby glade, which belonged to Kurpie family. The 1 km-long street ranges from Kościeliska and Nowotarska Streets to Witkiewicza Street. The Foluszowy Stream flows along the pavement. Krupówki is one of the best-known promenades and constitutes the trade centre of Zakopane. Here you can find numerous shops, restaurants, snack-bars, a post-office, galleries, and service points. Crowds of international tourists, street-booths, in-5-minutes caricatures – this is the picture of contemporary Krupówki.

The altars were sculpted by Wojciech Kułach Wawrzyńcok from Gliczarów. The Way of the Cross was painted on glass by a contemporary artist Ewelina Pęksowa.

Just behind the church and the chapel one can find an extraordinary place – „Pęksowy Brzyzek". It's an old cemetery. People were being buried besides the chapel, even before the cemetery was officially founded in mid XIXth century by Józef Stolarczyk (already mentioned above) on the grounds donated by Jan Pęksa. Initially all deceased were being buried here, as it was the only cemetery in Zakopane. However, after the death of Tytus Chałubiński in 1898 the cemetery became a resting place of the most prominent persons – artists, writers and members of honoured highlander families. The cemetery also hosts the ashes of great people, who died in other regions than the Tatra mountains and whose remains were brought to „Pęksowy Brzyzek" well after their deaths. There are also few symbolic tombstones for celebrities who died abroad. Among the buried here one can find famous writers – Kornel Makuszyński, Stanisław Witkiewicz and Kazimierz Przerwa Tetmajer, a poet – Władysław Orkan, a medicine doctor and botanist – Tytus Chałubiński, a storyteller – Jan Krzeptowski Sabała, an architect – Karol Stryjeński, a sculptor – Antonii Kenar, a sportswoman – Helena Marusarzówna, and father Józef Stolarczyk. There are also family tombstones of Chramcowie and Pawlikowscy families, along with symbolic crypts of Bronisław Czech and Mariusz Zaruski. Not only the names on grave stones are impressive, the vaults themselves are remarkable too. Some of them can be easily classified as works of art, and were made by such master craftsman like Stanisław Witkiewicz, Antoni Kenar, or Antoni Rząsa.

The confined space of the cemetery, squeezed in-between the busy Kościeliska Street and a stream of people rushing towards Gubałówka, or the marketplace, is so peaceful that coming back into the real world seems to be almost impossible.

*The Old Church of Virgin Mary from Częstochowa and st. Klemens on Kościeliska Street. It was built in 1847, and later extended. The altars were made by Wojciech Kułach, while The Way of the Cross was painted on glass by Ewelina Pęksowa. On the foreground you can see the chapel of the Gąsienice family.*

**The Old Cemetery on Pęksowy Brzyzek.** „Homeland is soil and graves. A nation that has lost its memory will loose its life. Zakopane remembers." These words were written on a plate hanging by the cemetery's entrance gate by father Jan Tobolak. The gate was designed by Stanisław Witkiewicz. The wall around the cemetery was built in the XIXth century, according to a project of father Józef Stolarczyk the first parish-priest of Zakopane. There are around 300 graves in this cemetery. They belong to members of highlander clans and people who's work was specially beneficial for Zakopane and the whole Tatra region.

Behind the „Old Church" stands the glamorous house of the Wnuki family (Kościeliska Street 8). It was constructed in 1850 and is one of the oldest buildings in Zakopane. Since it was the first building of such proportions in the town, it served as a culture center. It has a rich history. Its guest-lists include such names like Helena Modrzejewska, Tytus Chałubiński and Władysław Anczyc.

The original farm-yard of Gąsienice Nawsie family (Kościeliska Street 12) was build around 1850 by Jan Gąsienica Walczak.

The famous „Koliba" villa – the first building designed and built in Zakopiański style is under number 18. Currently it houses Stanisław Witkiewicz's Museum of Zakopiański Style. The structure was completed in 1894 after two years of construction work. It was built for Zygmunt Gnatowski, by Józef Kaspruś Socha and Maciej Gąsienica Józkowy. Initially the villa served as a pension, then it was a nursery and an orphanage.

Little further down the street, on the left, under number 15 we find the Art Lyceum of A. Kenar. Earlier this building was the home to „Strug" woodwork workshop and the School of Wood Industry. The houses of Gąsienice Bednarze family, built in 1880, stand on the right-hand side of Kościeliska Street under numbers 38 and 40.

Just beside them we see „Cicha" villa (earlier know as „Sobczakówka"). It was built before 1880 by the Gąsienice Sobczaki family. The villa was visited by Jan Kasprowicz, Maria Curie-Skłodowska and Stefan Żeromski.

Number 44 is the house of well known violin makers – the Marduls. Further on, number 52, the farm-yard of Gąsienice Sieczki family. J.I. Kraszewski, a famous Polish writer, lived here in 1866.

Our walk ends near the Chapel of the Pallotine Fathers – the Sanctuary of Virgin Mary of Fatima on Krzeptówki. The chapel is well worth seeing. It was built in 1957 inside a stylish villa. The interior is made of wood and is beautifully ornamented in the

*Koliba Villa on Kościeliska Street 18 was the first structure built according to Stanisław Witkiewicz's Zakopiański Style.*

*The chapel of the Pallotine Priests* on Krzeptówki – The Sanctuary of Virgin Mary from Fatima. It was set up in early 1950's in a highlander's house on Krzeptówki. The chapel was built in 1957. In mid-1970's it was upgraded to a church. In 1961 cardinal Stefan Wyszyński donated a cedar sculpture of Virgin Mary to the Pallotine Priests. The construction of a new church, designed by Stanisław Tylka, was initiated in 1987. It was created as a thanksgiving for protecting the life of Pope John Paul II in the 1981 assassination attempt.

highlanders' style. It was designed by father Mirosław Drozdek, while the craft work was done by Marian Styrczula Maśniak and Władysław Czop.

A walk along Kościeliska Street towards Krzeptówki is very interesting. Yet as the street is a very busy one, the excursion is not the most pleasant or peaceful.

## GUBAŁÓWKA

In the vicinity of the regional marketplace, on the protraction of Krupówki, we find the lower station of the scenic railway to Gubałówka. The installation was built in 1938. It is one of many tourist attractions in Zakopane. It is a fast mean of transport (around 5 minutes) to the top of Gubałówka (1120 m asl). The railroad is operational all year long carrying crowds of skiers during the Winter and comparable amounts of tourists in the Summer. Gubałówka can also be reached by foot, but such a walk takes around an hour. The mountain overlooks Zakopane from the North and is one of the most spectacular sight-seeing sites. From here you can marvel at the view of Zakopiańska Kotlina (Zakopane Dale) and the Tatra mountains. From the other side you can see Podhale. Thus, on a sunny day a trip to Gubałówka, on foot, or by rail, is worth making. On top of the mountain you will find a sight-seeing terrace, a few souvenir shops and small snack bars. While being here one ought to try the genuine ram shashlik. To your list of places worth-seeing you should probably add the interesting chapel of Virgin Mary's Eternal Aid. Build in 1971 it is shaped like a small wooden church, with austere and unusual interior. A popular route for short excursions is the foot-path from the upper station of the scenic railroad on Gubałówka in the direction of Butorowy Wierch and the chair-lift (30-40 minutes). The exceptional sights of both Tatra and Beskidy mountains on the opposite sides of the path, guarantee an unforgettable experience.

*The view from Gubałówka to the ridge above Dolina Gąsienicowa (Gąsienice Valley) ranging from Żółta Turnia (Yellow Crag), Granaty (Granades), Kozie Wierchy (Goat's Wierchy) to Kościelec • The station of the scenic railway to Gubałówka • Pasmo Gubałowskie (Gubałówka Belt) as seen from Równia Krupowa (Krupowa Plane).*

*A market. The Gubałówka Street is an extension of the lower part of Krupówki. The street leads to the lower station of the railway to Gubałówka. The largest regional market in Zakopane stretches along it. Here you can buy any souvenir you like, from a highlander's ornamented axe to a coat. You can also find things like forest-fruits, mushrooms, all kinds of cheeses, especially smoked ones. The former come in all shapes and sizes. They are made of sheep milk or rather a mixture of cow and sheep milk. Their specific taste is a complement of Zakopane's image.*

While riding the chair-lift down from Butorowy Wierch we can gaze at the picturesque sight of Tatra mountains and Zakopane. This relatively short excursion provides a number of attractions and is not very exhausting.

## KOŚCIELISKO

Kościelisko is a small town placed on the south slopes of the Gubałówka Belt, comprised of 21 settlements. The town center is located in Kire, while the most significant place is the Szeligówka, with its beautiful church of St. Casimir the Prince (1916).

The tradition and culture of the region has always been fostered in Kościelisko and hence the town is sometimes called „the heart of Podhale". Many prominent persons come from Kościelisko. This was the home-town of Jan Krzeptowski Sabała, Bartłomiej Obrochta, Andrzej Stopka Nazimek, Stanisław Nędza Kubiniec, Andrzej Tylka Suleja. Currently, Kościelisko is a typical holiday destination, with many hotels and rooms to rent. Because of its peacefulness the town attracts celebrities from all over the country, who wish to live away from the clatter of Zakopane.

*Kościelisko is closed from the South by Czerwone Wierchy (the Red Pinnacles) and lays on the Southern slopes of Gubałówka, Butorowy Wierch and Palenica Kościeliska. It is a splendid starting location for hiking in the Western Tatra and especially in Dolina Kościeliska (Kościeliska Valley) (Kiry) and Dolina Małej Łąki (Little Meadow Valley) • The plate of st. Casimir in front of the Church in Kościelisko.*

# THE TATRA MOUNTAINS

The Tatra mountains were shaped during millions of years by numerous factors including tectonic activity, glacier and post glacier phenomena, or geological transformations. They constitute our heritage, and as such deserve special care.

The national parks created on both the Polish and Slovak sides are divided by the countries' borders. The whole Tatra region covers the area of around 785 km². 610 km² on the Slovak side, and 175 km² are on the Polish side. The whole belt of Tatra mountains is divided into: Tatry Bielskie, Tatry Wysokie (the High Tatra), Tatry Zachodnie (the Western Tatra) with the group of Siwy Wierch (White Wierch) from Huciańska Przełęcz (Huciańska Pass – 905 m asl) on the West, to Zdziarska Przełęcz (Zdziarska Pass – 1077 m asl) on the East. The highest summit in the Tatra mountains is **Gierlach (2654 m asl)**, which lies in the Slovak part. The second highest mountain is **Łomnica (2634 m asl)**, then there is Lodowy Szczyt (Ice Summit – 2627 m asl), Durny Szczyt (Dumb Summit – 2623 m asl), Kopa Lodowa (Ice Pile – 261 m asl), Lawinowy Szczyt (Avalanche Summit – 2606 m asl) and Mały Gierlach (Small Gierlach – 2601 m asl). The highest summit on the Polish side is the North-western peak of Rysy. It is on the fifteenth place of the Tatra's height ranking and lies on the border. Other summits on the Polish side include: Mięguszowiecki Szczyt (Mięguszowiecki Summit – 2438 m asl), Niżnie Rysy (Lower Rysy – 2430 m asl), Czarny Mięguszowiecki Szczyt (Black Mięguszowiecki Summit – 2410 m asl) Pośredni Mięguszowiecki Szczyt (Middle Mięguszowiecki Summit – 2393 m asl), Cubryna (2373 m asl), Wołowa Turnia (Ox's Crag), Hińczowa Turnia (Hińczowa Crag), Żabia Turnia Mięguszowiecka (Frog's Mięguszowicka Crag) and Świnica (2301 m asl). The highest summit, that is entirelly on the Polish side is **Kozi Wierch (Goat's Wierch – 2291 m asl)**.

## TATRY BIELSKIE

The part of the Tatra mountains called „Tatry Bielskie" is build from calcium rocks and dolomites. It covers an area of over 67 km² and creates a 14 km long ridge between Zdzirska Przełęcz (Zdzirska Pass) and the Przełęcz pod Kopą (The Pass under the Pile – 1750 m asl) separating them from the High Tatra. The highest summits of Tatry Bielskie are: Hawrań (2152 m asl), Płaczliwa Skała (Whimpering Rock – 2142 m asl) and Szalony Wierch (Crazy Wierch – 2061 m asl)

Tatry Bielskie is a strict nature preserve, with limited tourist traffic. Numerous caves make this part of Tatra very specific. Among them are: Jaskinie Bielskie (Bielskie Caves) and Jaskinia Alabastrowa (Alabaster Cave). The main starting point for most excursions is Ždiár on the path from Łysa Polana (Bold Glade) to Tatrzańska Łomnica.

## TATRY WYSOKIE (THE HIGH TATRA)

This part of the Tatra mountains is built from granite and covers an area of 335 km², from the Przełęcz pod Kopą to Liliowe Przełęcz (Saddle of Lilies – 1952 m asl), which separates the High Tatra from the Western Tatra. The highest summits of the High Tatra, being the highest summits of all Tatra mountains, have been already listed above.

## TATRY ZACHODNIE (THE WESTERN TATRA)

The Western Tatra mountains stretch Westwards from Liliowe Przełęcz (The Pass of Lilies) to the group of Siwy Wierch (White Wierch – 1805 m asl). The strict nature preserve ends in Huciańska Przełęcz (Huciańska Pass) and covers an area of nearly 400 km². The mountains are built mainly of calcium rocks, dolomites and crystalic slates. The rounded tops of the lower mountains, covered with grass, often end with precipices.

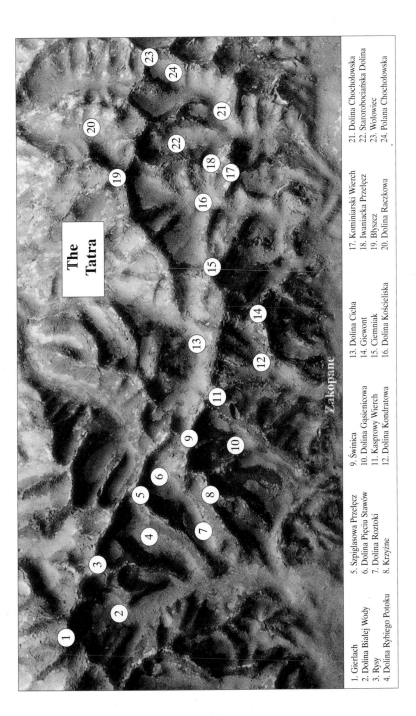

# The Tatra

1. Gierlach
2. Dolina Białej Wody
3. Rysy
4. Dolina Rybiego Potoku
5. Szpiglasowa Przełęcz
6. Dolina Pięciu Stawów
7. Dolina Roztoki
8. Krzyżne
9. Świnica
10. Dolina Gąsienicowa
11. Kasprowy Wierch
12. Dolina Kondratowa
13. Dolina Cicha
14. Giewont
15. Ciemniak
16. Dolina Kościeliska
17. Kominiarski Wierch
18. Iwaniacka Przełęcz
19. Błyszcz
20. Dolina Raczkowa
21. Dolina Chochołowska
22. Starorobociańska Dolina
23. Wołowiec
24. Polana Chochołowska

Zakopane

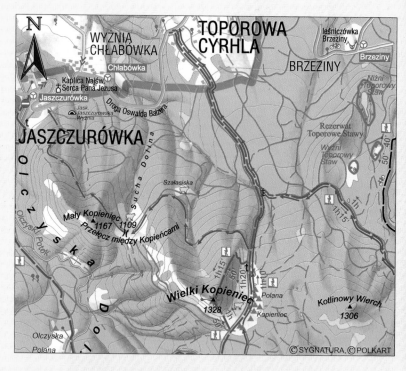

*Dolina Olczyska (Olczyska Valley) – Wielki Kopieniec (Great Kopieniec)*

The highest summit of the Western Tatra is Bystra (2248 m asl), which lies on the Slovak side. The main ridge of the massif contains smaller mountains like Kasprowy Wierch (1987 m asl), Czuba Goryczkowa (1913 m asl), Kopa Kondracka (2005 m asl), Małołączniak (2096 m asl), Krzesanica (2122 m asl), Ciemniak (2096 m asl), Starorobociański Wierch (2176 m asl), Kończysty Wierch (2002 m asl) and Wołowiec (2064 m asl).

Droga pod Reglami (**The Road under Prealpes**) leads along the edge of Tatra National Park. From this walkway you can reach all the valleys, which lay in direct vicinity of Zakopane and Kościelisko. At the entrances to the valleys you will usually find parking-lots for cars and mini-buses. Another major foot-path, called Ścieżka nad Reglami (Path over Prealpes) stretches above Droga pod Reglami. This track intersects with the valleys and hence acts as a link between them. It is marked with black colour.

## JASZCZURÓWKA AND TOPOROWA CYRHLA

A walk to Jaszczurówka is worth recommending. It can be reached from the center of Zakopane in about one hour, or from Kuźnickie Rondo in roughly fifteen minutes. Jaszczurówka is a complex of summer villas. Hot springs were discovered here in the first half of the XIXth century. In Jaszczurówka-Bory you will find the St. Ursula nunnery and a chapel with a beautiful larch altar, dated 1938. Karol Wojtyła in his times as a bishop was a frequent guest in the nunnery.

The chapel of The Holy Jesus' Heart is also an interesting landmark. It stands by the road to Morskie Oko. Founded in 1908 by the Uznańscy family. The structure, designed by Stanisław Witkiewicz, is a prime example of Zakopiański Style in a sacral building. The wooden construction stands on a tall stone foundation. From the outside it is covered with lavish ornaments, while having a simple and crude interior. The roof is made from shingles decorated with distinctive signatures. Above the entrance hangs a small sculpture of Jesus Christ, made

*The chapel in Jaszczurówka.*
*A wooden chapel of The Saint Jesus' Heart.*

by Józef Janos from Dębno. The main altar, made of sycamore and ash wood, is the most noteworthy part of the interior. It is formed in the shape of a typical front wall of a highlander's hut. The main altar is accompanied by two side stained-glass panels. The first one, picturing Virgin Mary from Częstochowa and the emblem of Polish Eagle, while the second depicts Virgin Mary from Ostra Brama and the Lithuanian national emblem. Thanks to precise renovation, completed in the beginning of 1980's, the chapel can be seen in all its magnificence.

From Jaszczurówka you can walk to Dolina Olczyska (Olczyska Valley – 2 km away, approx. 40 minutes) and further, to Kopieniec (1328 m asl – 1,5 hour).

**Dolina Olczyska** covers an area of 4,5 km². It is well known due to a krastic underground stream outlet, which is one of the largest of its kind in Tatra. The stream is called Potok Olczyski (Olczyski Stream). Walking down the slope, through a glade, you will soon reach Polana Kopieniec (Kopieniec Glade 1210-1260 m asl). Here you will find shacks and sheepherders with their animals. From here you may walk to Wielki Kopieniec (1328 m asl) and marvel at beautiful views. Then, down to Toporowa Cyrhla (approx. 40 min.) and head for Zakopane by foot or by bus. Toporowa Cyrhla is a typical tourist village. It covers a significant area between Hrubiański Potok (the Hrubiański Stream) and Olczański Wierch. This place was once a sheepherders' settlement. The local church is one of the more interesting structures here.

A nice foot-path (approx. 2 hours) leads from Toporowa Cyrhla to Polana Waksmundzka (Waksmundzka Glade: 1400-1440 m asl), through Psia Trawka (Dog's Grass – 1183 m asl). Another pleasant path will take you to Sucha Woda (Dry Water) and further along the feet of Suchy Wierch (Dry Wierch – 1485 m asl) and Ostry Wierch (Sharp Wierch – 1475 m asl) to the vast Waksmundzka Polana (Waksmundzka Glade). From here it is worth walking up a little further (15 min) to Równia Waksmundzka (Waksmundzka Plane – 1440 m asl) and, to Gęsia Szyja (Goose Neck – 1490 m asl) – only 20 min more. This short walk is worth taking especially

*Toporowa Cyrhla • A view of the High Tatra • The new church on Toporowa Cyrhla.*

*Dolina Olczyska* (Olczyska Valley) lays above Jaszczurówka, South from the road to Morskie Oko. It is encircled by Nosal, Skupniów Upłaz (from which you can see the whole valley), Wielka Królowa Kopa (Great Queen Pile) and, from the East, by Wielki Kopieniec and Mały Kopieniec (lower picture). The first part of the path, to Polana Olczyska (Olczyska Glade), leads along Potok Olczyski (the Olczyski Stream). The stream flows from an outlet of an underground stream on the edge of the glade.

on a sunny, clear day, as the view from Gęsia Szyja is breathtaking. From here you can see both Tatry Wysokie and Tatry Bialskie. The return route to Cyrhla takes around 2,5 hour.

## PREALP VALLEYS

### Droga pod Reglami (Road under Prealpes)

Road under Prealpes starts by Murowanica near Księżówka, above Rondo Kuźnickie and leads along the boundary of Tatra National Park. The road seems almost designed for pleasure walks. Walking along it, you will find entrance gates to numerous valleys including: Dolina Białego (the Valley of the White – it can also be reached from Piłsudski or Bronka Czecha streets in Zakopane), Dolina ku Dziurze (the Valley towards the Hole – can be reached from Zakopane, Kasprusie Street, through Strążyska Street and Droga do Daniela (Road to Daniel)), Dolina Strążyska (Strążyska Valley – again through Strążyska Street), Dolina za Bramką (the Valley behind the Gate – can be reached through Krzeptówki), Dolina Małej Łąki (the Valley of a Small Meadow – through Gronik), Staników Żleb (Staników Gully – through Nędzówka), Dolina Kościeliska (Kościeliska Valley – through Kiry), Dolina Lejowa (Crater Valley – through Biały Potok), Dolina Chochołowska (Chochołów Valley – through Siwa Polana).

It takes 3 hours to walk the whole 13 km-long Droga pod Reglami (Road under Prealpes). To the most distant part of the road, i.e. Dolina Chochołowska (Chochołów Valley), you should probably take a mini-bus, and then walk to Zakopane.

### Ścieżka nad Reglami (The Path above Prealpes)

The path is marked with black colour. It leads from Kalatówki to Dolina Chochołowska (Chochołów Valley). The total distance of this foot-path is over 16 km and it takes more than 5 hours to walk. Kalatówki can be reached by road from Kuźnice (30 minutes walking). The black trail turns into the forest before the Kalatówki hotel.

*Dolina Olczyska (Olczyska Valley).*
*The green trail to Wielki Kopieniec through Dolina Olczyska.*

## Dolina Białego (The Valley of the White)

A 1 h 15 min walk from Droga pod Reglami (Road under Prealpes) along the yellow trail.

Dolina Białego (2,5 km long, area of 3 km²) begins near **Krokwia** (1378 m asl), **Sarnia Skała** (Deer's Rock – 1377 m asl) and Suchy Wierch (Dry Wierch – 1539 m asl) and goes all the way to Wrótki (1580 m asl) – a pass on the Eastern slope of Giewont. The area of the whole valley is a strict nature preserve. Beech- and fir-tree forests, numerous dolomite rocks, Biały Potok (the White Stream) with small bridges, make the valley one of the most beautiful in this area. Thus it is frequently visited by large groups of tourists. The yellow trail in the upper part of Dolina Białego converges with the black trail of Ścieżka nad Reglami (Path over Prealpes). It takes 50 min to walk from this junction to Strążyska or 1 h 20 min, in the opposite direction, to Kalatówki.

## Dolina ku Dziurze (Valley towards the Hole)

A 25-minute-long walk from Droga pod Reglami (Road under Prealpes) along the black trail.

The valley, placed between Spaleniec and Grześkówka, only 1,6 km long, ends with a cave called **Dziura** (The Hole). The cave was made by an underground stream, which drilled a calcium block, a part of a larger dolomite rock. Dziura has two parts, a vestibule and a 30 metre long main chamber. It is the nearest and the most available cave in the vicinity of Zakopane. It is especially popular among school groups. If you choose to enter the cave, don't forget to take a flashlight.

*Przysłop Miętusi (upper photo)* • *Dolina Małej Łąki (Small Meadow Valley – lower photo)* • *On the side: the entrance to Dolina Białego (the Valley of the White) from Droga pod Reglami (The Path below Prealpes).*

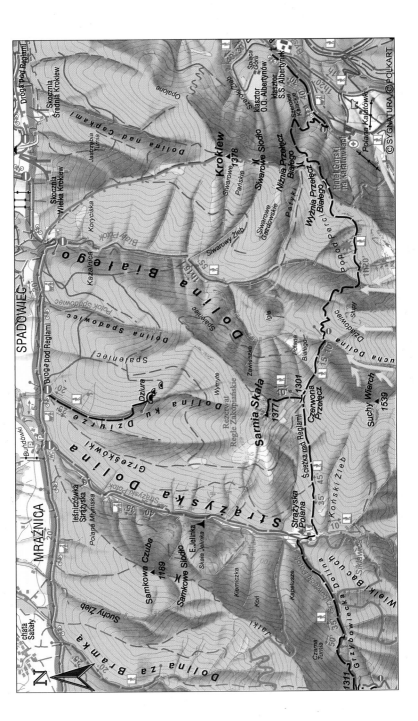

## Dolina Strążyska (Strążyska Valley)

A 40-minute-long walk from Droga pod Reglami (Road under Prealpes) along the red trail.

Dolina Strążyska, a prolongation of Strążyska street, is one of the most frequented by tourists valleys. It is often used for acclimatisation of newcomers, or for pleasure-walks in-between high-mountain excursions. The valley is located between Samkowa Czuba, Łysanki, **Grzybowiec** and Sarnia Skała (Deer's Rock) with Suchy Wierch (Dry Wierch).

On entering the valley you will see Leśniczówka Strążyska (Strążyska Forester's Lodge) on your right. The glade, it stands on, is called Polana Młyniska (Mill Glade). The trail in this part of the valley leads through a beech-tree forest. This is especially beautiful during the golden Polish Autumn. From here you will be accompanied by a stream called **Strążyski Potok (the Strążyski Stream)**. It flows quickly in a deep dent. The foot-path crosses the stream in few places. Along the track you will also find a large rock with a commemorating plate and a bust of a Czech – Edward Jelinek (the rock was also named after him). Another interesting landmark is the group of marvellous **Kominy Strążyskie (Strążyskie Chimneys)** – sharp dolomite crags.

After reaching a glade on your right hand side, you will see a small bridge. It carries the black and red trails across the stream. The former leads to Dolina Małej Łąki (The Small Meadow Valley – 1 h 10 min), while the latter to Giewont (2 h 30 min). But first both colours will take you to Przełęcz w Grzybowcu (the Saddle in Grzybowiec – 1311 m asl – 50 min).

On the wide Polana Strążyska (Strążyska Glade) you will find a couple of sheepherders' shacks. In one of them you can buy a genuine apple cake.

The yellow trail leads, above the glade and along the stream, to **Siklawica** (1100 m asl). The water falls from a ledge of Mała Dolinka (Small Valley) under Giewont, which closes Dolina Strążyska (Strążyska Valley) from the South. Siklawica is a set of two 12 metre high waterfalls, located one over the other. Together they create the main current of the Strążyski Stream.

*The meadows of bolt valleys • This cave is the destination point of the tourist trail through Dolina ku Dziurze (the Valley towards the Hole).*

**Dolina za Bramką (Valley behind the Gate)**

A 25-minute-long walk from Droga pod Reglami (the Road under Prealpes) along the green trail.

Setting off from Zakopane we head for Krzeptówki. Here, just opposite the entrance to the valley, stands a XVIIIth century farmyard. It once belonged to Jan Krzeptowski Sabała. This structure is regarded as one of the most interesting specimens of Highlander architecture.

Dolina za Bramką (the Valley behind the Gate) is approximately 2 km long and leads through narrow, rock gates. Dolomite rocks on the Western side and Jasiowe Turnie (Jasiowe Crags) on the right side of the valley underline the unique charm of this place. The trail ends suddenly with no special landmark. You return along the same path.

**Dolina Małej Łąki (Little Meadow Valley)**

A one-hour-long walk from Droga pod Reglami (Road under Prealpes) along the yellow trail.

Dolina Małej Łąki is the smallest post-glacier valley in the Polish Tatra, which has the classical U-shaped cross-section. It is 5 km long and built of dolomites, calcium and sedimentary rocks. Initially it leads along Małołącki Potok (the Little Meadow Stream), through a forest, then the trail reaches Wielka Polana Małołącka (The Great Małołącka Glade – 1175 m asl). By a large calcium stone Ścieżka nad Reglami (Path above Prealpes) appears and heads for Przysłop Miętusi and further to Dolina Kościeliska (1 h 10 min). In the opposite direction the path leads to Dolina Strążyska (Strążyska Valley – 1 hour).

The magnificent glade is closed with a perfectly visible crag of Giewont and Czerwone Wierchy. It is one of the most beautiful glades in all Tatra and has very diversified geological structures and plant life. The yellow trail leads from the upper level of the glade to Kondracka Przełęcz (Kondracka Saddle – 1725 m asl – 1 h 30 min). The map of this terrain can be found on page 145.

*Dolina Strążyska (Strążyska Valley).*
*Strążyska glade and the highlander snack-bar • Siklawica waterfall.*

# Trzy doliny (The three valleys)

The lower parts of the three valleys: Dolina Roztoki (Roztoka Valley), Dolina Rybiego Potoku (the Fish' Stream Valley) and Dolina Pięciu Stawów Polskich (The Valley of Five Polish Ponds), are located at the junction of Rybi Potok (the Fish' Stream) and Biała Woda (White Water).

The glaciers, making their way back due North, thousands of years ago, created great moraines, upcasts and rifts.

The hard ice dug valleys, formed summits and crests, while the streams of water coming down from the melting glaciers shaped the lakes. The ice moved lower and lower. It was followed by water and more ice, which cut through moraines and massive walls. These processes were responsible for the creation of the Tatra ponds, with their shapes stretched out along the glacier's path. The three valleys were crammed between granite ridges. In those days mysterious, today they have their names.

**Dolina Rybiego Potoku** (the Fish' Stream Valley) is surrounded by the ridge of Żabie (Frog's) from the East, by Rysy and Mięguszowieckie Szczyty (Mięguszowieckie Summits) from the South and by the ridges of Miedziany Wierch (Copper Wierch) and Opalony Wierch from the West. **Dolina Białej Wody** (White Water Valley), with the massif of Młynarz (the Miller), lies on the Slovak side, separated from Rybi Potok by Żabie. **Biała Woda** begins its flow on the slopes of Gierlach as a minor stream. Heading down, for Białka, it grows to become a significant river, flowing along the bottom of the valley. As we walk down the path to Morskie Oko, we witness the whole transformation.

Miedzine (Copper) with Opalone rise above **Dolina Pięciu Stawów Polskich** (The Valley of Five Polish Ponds). On the opposite side, the valley is closed by the ridges of Kozie Wierchy (Goat's Wierchy) and Świnica with Liptowskie Mury (Liptowskie Walls). From the North, Dolina Pięciu Stawów Polskich is carved by a granite threshold of Stawiarska Ściana (Stawiarska Wall), with its Wielka Siklawa (Great Siklawa) waterfall, dropping down into the Roztoka Stream. **Dolina Roztoki** (Roztoka Valley) was craved between the massif of Wołoszyn and the steep rocky slopes of Opalone.

## Palenica Białczańska

The three valleys can be reached by car. From Zakopane you can take one of two roads. The first one will take you through Bukowina Tatrzańska and Głodówka. The second is the Oswald Balzer road and leads through Jaszczurówka and Toporowa Cyrhla (Oswald Balzer was a lawyer, who at the turn of the century won a court case against Hungarians, who wanted ownership rights of Morskie Oko). Both roads end with a barrier, marking the border of Tatrzański Park Narodowy (Tatra National Park), and a parking-lot on **Palenica Białczańska**. Yet the easiest, and probably the cheapest means of transport are the mini-buses, which set off from the bus station in Zakopane. The drivers will take you to Palenica Białczańska and will later wait till the last tourist comes back, to take them to Zakopane.

In Palenica Białczańska is the entrance to the Tatra National Park. In order to enter the park you need to buy a ticket. After purchasing the ticket you can begin your trek, surrounded by a group of other tourists heading for Morskie Oko. You should reach your destination after approximately 2 hours (9 km). The path to Morskie Oko is practically a paved road and is utterly boring. Instead of walking you can choose to take a carriage (or sledge in Winter). It will take you to the old car-park on Włosienica. The distance from

here to Morskie Oko is only 1.5 km. The ride takes around one hour and costs less on the way down. The carriage with up to twenty tourists is pulled by two horses and quickly overtakes those who decided to walk, attracting envious looks.

Various trails separate from the road to Morskie Oko:
– The blue trail begins near Palenica and leads to **Rusinowa Polana** (Rusinowa Glade). The walk takes about 50 minutes. There are two routes to choose when walking back to Zakopane from Rusinowa Polana. The first one will take you through Złota Polana (Golden Glade) to the road on Zazadnia (1 h). The second possibility is to take the green trail through **Gęsia Szyja** (Goose's Neck) to Waksmundzka Równia (Waksmundzka Plane). From here you can take the red trail to Toporowa Cyrhla (total time: 1 h 40 min).
– The red trail, which sets off just before Wodogrzmoty Mickiewicza (Mickiewicz' Waterfalls), leads to Polana pod Wołoszynem (The Glade under Wołoszyn – 30 min) and further on through Waksmundzka Polana to Toporowa Cyrhla (above 3 hours).

The two trails are linked by the green trail, which connects Waksmundzka Polana (Waksmundzka Glade) and Rusinowa Polana (Rusinowa Glade) via Gęsia Szyja (Goose's Neck – 1490 m asl – approx. 1 h – the trail leads through forests and dwarf-mountain-pines to arrive at a grassy summit).

**The road to Wodogrzmoty Mickiewicza (Mickiewicz Waterfalls)**
The road to Morskie Oko winds on the way up above the river Biała Woda (**White Water**), which flows on the Slovak side. After 40 minutes of walking from Roztoka forester's lodge you will reach a bridge (over the Roztoka Stream), from which you can see Wodogrzmoty Mickiewicza (Mickiewicz Waterfalls).

*Roztoka (1030 m asl).*
    *Wincenty Pol's tourist hostel on Polana Roztoka (Roztoka Glade). It was built at the turn of XIXth century by the old road to Morskie Oko.*

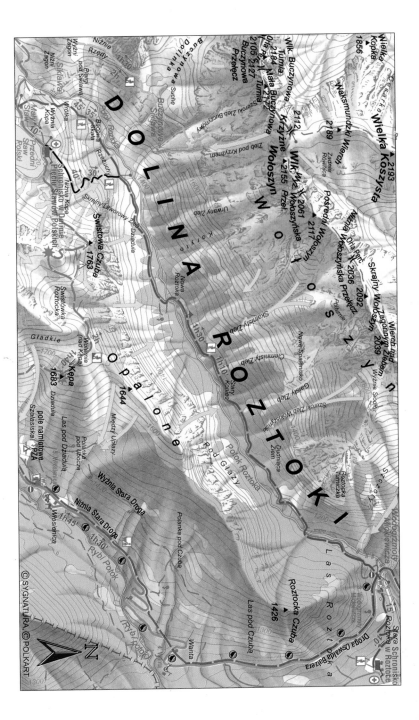

# Dolina Roztoki (Roztoka Valley)

**Wodogrzmoty Mickiewicza** (Mickiewicz Waterfalls). The water from Wielki Staw (the Great Pond) in Dolina Pięciu Stawów Polskich (The Valley of Five Polish Ponds), meets two great rock thresholds on its path. The first one is the threshold of Stawiarska Ściana (Stawiarska Wall) in the upper part of Dolina Roztoki (Roztoka Valley), where Wielka Siklawa (Great Siklawa) starts. The second, located in the lower part of the valley, where a narrowing of rocks, between Wołoszyn and Roztocka Czuba creates a series of waterfalls and cascades called Wodogrzmoty Mickiewicza (Mickiewicz Waterfalls – 1099 m asl). The group was divided into three sets: Wyżni (Upper), Pośredni (Middle) and Niźni (Lower). The threshold and Wodogrzmot' Pośredni (Middle Waterfall) are clearly visible from the bridge, but the rest of Wodogrzmoty cannot be seen from the trail. Below the waterfall, Potok Roztoki joins the Białka river.

The green trail from the former car-park leads to **Schronisko Roztoka** im. Wincentego Pola (Wincenty Pol's Roztoka Hostel – 1031 m asl) on Stara Roztoka glade. The cosy hostel is set back from the main tourist trails and is an ideal starting point for excursions into the three valleys.

## Along Dolina Roztoki (Roztoka Valley)

A 2-hour-long walk through Wodogrzmoty (Mickiewicz Waterfalls), Nowa Roztoka (New Roztoka) and Wielka Siklawa (Great Siklawa) along the green trail.

The green trail leading along Dolina Roztoki towards Dolina Pięciu Stawów Polskich (The Valley of Five Polish Ponds) originates by the bridge over Wodogrzmoty Mickiewicza (Mickiewicz Waterfalls). The trail initially goes through the valley between

*Dolina Roztoka (Roztoka Valley).*
*The upper parts of Dolina Roztoka • A tourist path among dwarf-mountain-pines (the photo on the right). The walls of Wołoszyn massif are visible in the foreground.*

**Dolina Roztoka.**

The lower part of Dolina Roztoki between the steep walls of Opalony ridge and the massif of Wołoszyn, that falls into the valley with numerous avalanche gullies.

The wooden bridge enables the crossing of Potok Roztoki. The water flows to Wodogrzmoty Mickiewicza (Mickiewicz Waterfalls). Then, it falls into the Białka river in Stara Roztoka (Old Roztoka). The stream is one of many, which together create Dunajec.

À shack by the green trail, that leads through Dolina Roztoki. It can serve as a shelter if the weather deteriorates.

43

the great massif of Wołoszyn and Roztocka Czuba (1426 m asl). Then through the ridge of Opalony (1644 m asl) and Świstowa Czuba (1736 m asl) in its upper part. Avalanches come down the ridge during the Winter. They can even reach Wodogrzmoty. The trail leads through a forest (spruces and stone pines) along Potok Roztoka (the Roztoka Stream). After around 40 min, you will pass a glade called Nowa Roztoka (1300 m asl). After crossing a stream the forest slowly gives ground to dwarf mountain pines.

The black trail appears. It leads to a hostel on Przedni Staw (the Frontal Pond – 40 min) omitting Wielka Siklawa.

We reach the threshold of Stawiarska Ściana (Stawiarska Wall) overlooked by Dolinka Buczynowa (Beech Valley) and the ridge of Wielka Buczynowa Turnia (Great Beech Crag – 2184 m asl) above. On the opposite side lays the dale of Świstówka Roztocka in the ridge of Opalony Wierch (2115 m asl). We are now standing on Wrótki, a rock saddle. The largest waterfall in the Tatra mountains, **Wielka Siklawa** (Great Siklawa), towers in front of us.

Wielka Siklawa is a group of several, parallel cascades. They are propelled by water coming down from Wielki Staw Polski (Great Polish Pond) through a smooth post-glacier threshold of Stawiarska ściana from the height of 1620-1580 m. The waterfall is almost 70 metres long with a 30 degrees slope. The water from this waterfall propels, the yet very immature, Roztoki Stream. The stream, in turn, after 7 km reaches Wodogrzmoty (Mickiewicz Waterfalls) and reinforces Białka.

Further, the green trail leads along Wielka Siklawa, through wet rocks, to Mały Staw (the Small Pond). Here it joins the blue trail coming from Zawrat and heads for a hostel by Przedni Staw.

*Stawiarska Ściana (Stawiarska Wall) and Staw Przedni (the Frontal Pond).*
*On the photo you can see the blue trail from Morskie Oko to Dolina Pięciu Stawów Polskich (The Valley of Five Polish Ponds).*
*The photo on the right: Potok Roztoki (Roztoka Stream).*

**Wielka Siklawa** (Great Siklawa)

On the photos you can see the upper part of Dolina Roztoki, between Świstowa Czuba (1763 m asl) and the walls of Wielki Wołoszyn (2155 m asl).

The strong current of the water flowing from the Great Pond in Dolina Pięciu Stawów Polskich (The Valley of Five Polish Ponds) runs into a rock threshold of Stawiarska Ściana. The water falls from it into Dolina Roztoki along smoothened granite rocks with a couple of cascades on its way. This is Wielka Siklawa (1580-1620 m asl) – the largest waterfall in Poland. Its waters create Potok Roztoki (the Roztoka Stream).

# Dolina Rybiego Potoku (The Valley of Fish' Stream)

**Wodogrzmoty Mickiewicza (Mickiewicz's Waterfalls) – Morskie Oko.**

A 1-hour- 45-minute-long walk from Dolina Rybiego Potoku, through Włosienica and a moraine over Morskie Oko along the red trail.

The trail to Morskie Oko from Wodogrzmoty (Mickiewicz' Waterfalls) leads along a road. On numerous occasions you will encounter shortcuts, which omit wide curves of the paved road, but we advise you to stay on the track and save energy. After all you are heading for Rysy.

By the road you will see information plates with maps showing your location and giving information on the surrounding panorama. They may prove to be of some help.

We are now in the lower part of Dolina Rybiego Potoku (the Fish' Stream Valley), among forests covering Wołoszyn and Opalone, with Białka flowing on the Slovak side. By Want (1165 m asl, the beginning of zigzags) we pass Leśniczówka Morskie Oko (Morskie Oko Forester's Lodge). Beneath, Rybi Potok (the Fish' Stream) meets Biała Woda (White Water), creating **Białka**. Through the trees you can see summits with the massif of Młynarz (The Miller – 2170 m asl) overlooking Żabia Dolina (Frog's Valley).

*The ridge of Tatra above Morskie Oko from the South side: (from the left) the walls of Żabi Niżni Szczyt (Lower Frog's Summit), Niżnie Rysy (Lower Rysy – 2430 m asl) and Rysy (2499 m asl) in the mist, Żabia Przełęcz (Frog's Pass – 2225 m asl), Żabi Koń (Frog's Horse – 2291 m asl), Wołowa Turnia (Ox's Crag – 2373 m asl) and further the ridge to Mięguszowieckie Szczyty (Mięguszowieckie Summits).*

*The wall of Kazalnica is on the right. Czarny Staw (the Black Pond) below Rysy lays behind the visible rock threshold. In the middle of the photo you can see Bula pod Rysami. The red trail to Rysy leads through it.*

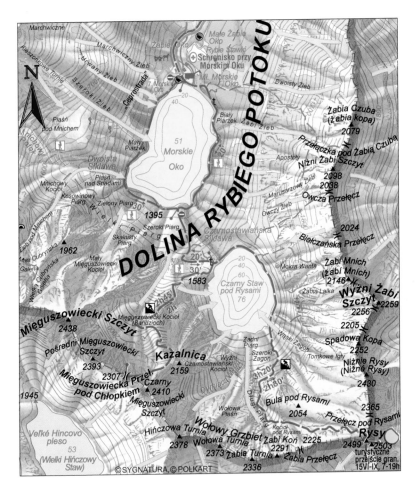

**Włosienica** (1310 m asl) is a large, paved clearing in a forest. Here the carriage ride ends and walking begins. The carriages turn back and wait for returning tourists below the clearing. Earlier, Włosienica was a large parking-lot with all its consequences to the natural environment. A Winter shelter and a relatively large restaurant are the only constructions on the glade. The track from Włosienica to Morskie Oko is 1,6 km long. A path turning to the right from the track leads to a mountaineers' base on Szałasiska glade. It is available only to the members of the Polish Mountaineer Association.

The slopes of Opalony Wierch tower above the road. Great avalanches come down these slopes in the wintertime and often bury the road to Morskie

Oko. On the left, a group of small ponds (Żabie Oko (Frog's Eye), Rybie Stawki (the Fish' Ponds) and the last Małe Morskie Oko, a strict nature preserve). The steep ridge of Mnich (The Monk), sinister walls of Cubryna and Mięguszowieckie Szczyty (Mięguszowieckie Summits) will be visible as long as you stay in the vicinity of Morskie Oko. The blue trail, through Świstówka to Dolina Pięciu Stawów Polskich (2 h), branches off to the right as you pass the small ponds. We reach the terminal moraine. Beside the old manoeuvre-field for carriages stands an old wooden hostel – a former coach-house built at the end of the XIXth century, renovated and adapted to tourists' needs. The yellow trail starts opposite to the old hostel. It leads to Szpiglasowa Przełęcz (Szpiglasowa Pass) and Wrota Chałubińskiego (Chałubiński's Doors) (the trail turns red in Dolina za Mnichem (Valley behind the Monk)).

We are now in the post-glacier dale of **Morskie Oko**. Before us stands the hostel of Stanisław Staszic. It was built on the crest of a moraine, 1405 m asl. The structure is well visible from most trails leading through the dales of Morskie Oko and Czarny Staw (the Black Pond). Usually in front of the hostel you can see a colourful crowd of tourists. The lake is the most popular destination among tourists and hence the hostel is crowded. Inside you will find a restaurant. You can also make use of the field-glass on the porch and watch mountaineers climbing.

*Włosienica (1310 m asl) – a large clearing in the forest. It used to be a parking-lot, now it marks the end of a carriage ride from Palenica Białczańska. A winter shelter stands in the middle of the glade, while on its outskirts you can find a large snack-bar. After 30 minutes of walking from Włosienica you reach Morskie Oko.*

# The dale of Morskie Oko

The dale of Morskie Oko is a post-glacier structure shaped thousands of years ago, when the ice, which gathered in the dale, spilled over and moved downwards with the receding glacier creating a moraine rock threshold and further down forming Dolina Rybiego Potoku (the Fish' Stream Valley). Masses of ice coming down from Kotlina Czarnego Stawu joined those, which lay in the dale of Morskie Oko and spilled over a 200 metre high threshold. It was an enormous destructive force, which also carried a creative potential.

The dale is surrounded by granite summits. From the East by the ridge of Żabi and Żabi Szczyt Niżni (Frog's and Frog's Lower Summit – 2259 m asl). Further, Niżnie Rysy (Lower Rysy – 2430 m asl), which conceal the Polish highest summit, **Rysy** (2499 m asl). From the South the dale is closed by Żabia Przełęcz (Frog's Pass – 2225 m asl), the sharp crag of Żabi Koń (Frog's Horse – not a misprint – 2291 m asl) and of Wołowy Grzbiet (Ox's Rib) with Wołowa Turnia (Ox's Crag – 2373 m asl), Hińczowa Turnia (Hińczowa Crag – 2378 m asl), which is not visible from the hostel, Mięguszowieckie Szczyty (Mięguszowieckie Summits) including Czarny Mięguszowiecki Szczyt (The Black Mięguszowiecki Summit – 2410 m asl), **Mięguszowiecka Przełęcz pod Chłopkiem** (Mięguszowiecki Pass below the Peasant), Mięguszowiecki Szczyt

*The old hostel (a former couch-house) by Morskie Oko.*
*The photograph on the right depicts Cubryna (2376 m asl) and Mnich (The Monk) as seen from the road to Morskie Oko.*

(Mięguszowiecki Summit – 2393 m asl) separated with Hińczowa Przełęcz (Hińczowa Pass – 2323 m asl) from Cubryna (2376 m asl), which in turn overlooks the peak of Mnich. From the West, you can see the massif of Miedziany (Copper – 2233 m asl), and further to the North, Opalony Wierch (2115 m asl) and the ridge of Opalone ranging towards the base of Dolina Rybiego Potoku (the Fish' Stream Valley).

## Morskie Oko lake

Morskie Oko, in the past called Rybi Staw (the Fish' Pond) or Jezioro (The Lake), is located at the altitude of 1395 m asl inside a post-glacier dale. The terminal moraine, formed thousands of years ago, keeps the water of the lake within a rock niche 50,8 m deep. The greatest distance between two opposite points of the shore is 862 m, while the shortest is 566 m.

The water from the lake spills over the moraine on its Eastern side thus creating Rybi Potok (the Fish Stream), and several minor ponds visible from the road. In terms of area, Morskie Oko is comparable with Wielki Staw (the Great Pond) located in the neighbouring Dolina Pięciu Stawów Polskich (The Valley of Five Polish Ponds). They both cover around 34,5 ha and are the largest lakes in the Tatra mountains.

*Morskie Oko.*
*Sunbathing on a bench in front of the hostel • The view of the landscape around Morskie Oko with a stone pine.*

There is a track leading **around Morskie Oko**. It is 2600 m long and runs around the shore of the lake, so you can clearly see its bottom, covered with rocks just by the shoreline, or with sand if you look further. In the clean waters of Morskie Oko you can spot a trout, or other fish. We walk among dwarf mountain pines. Sometimes a stone pine appears, but with height they become very rare.

The 1000 metre-high rocks of Mięguszowieckie Szczyty (Mięguszowieckie Summits) tower above Morskie Oko. Their image reflects in the lake's peaceful waters.

In the old days, there was a tourist boat shuttling through the lake from the hostel to the opposite shore. During the Winter the lake is covered with a thick layer of ice. Sometimes, after large snowfalls, when the dales above Morskie Oko fill up with snow, avalanches come down onto the lake, crushing the ice and everything else in their path. Occasionally the shockwave caused by an avalanche hits the windows of the hostel making them clutter. The avalanche gullies and dales are well visible from Morskie Oko. Here we have Kocioł Mięguszowiecki (Mięguszowiecki Dale) – Bańdzioch, hanging between Pośredni Mięguszowiecki Szczyt (Middle Mięguszowiecki Summit) and the Northern wall of Mięguszowiecki Szczyt, Wielka Galeria Cubryńska (the Great Cubryńska Gallery) under Cubryna, Mały Kocioł Mięguszowiecki (Small Mięguszowiecki Dale) and Żleb pod Mnichem (The Gully under the

*Stanisław Staszic's hostel on the terminal moraine above Morskie Oko. You can see the tourist track running around the lake.*

**The summits of the upper ridge of High Tatra encircling Morskie Oko.** *On the upper photo you can see Mnich (The Monk – 2070 m asl, on the right lays Dolina za Mnichem, with the red trail leading to Chałubiński's Doors), Cubryna (2376 m asl. Below lays Wielka Galeria Cubryńska (Great Cubryn Gallery)), Przełęcz Hińczowa (Hińczowa Pass – 2323 m asl) and Mięguszowiecki Szczyt (Mięguszowiecki Summit – 2438 m asl).*

*The bottom photo: Przełęcz Hińczowa and Mięguszowiecki Szczyt, Wyżnia Przełęcz Mięguszowiecka (Upper Mięguszowiecka Pass – 2330 m asl), Pośredni Szczyt Mięguszowiecki (Middle Mięguszowiecki Summit – 2393 m asl, Kocioł Mięguszowiecki (Mięguszowiecki Dale) and Bańdzioch lay below), Przełęcz Mięguszowiecka pod Chłopkiem (Mięguszowiecka Pass below The Peasant – 2307 m asl) and Czarny Szczyt Mięguszowiecki (Black Mięguszowiecki Summit – 2410 m asl).*

Monk). The motion of snow-avalanches and sometimes, of much smaller rock-avalanches, created the conical **Wielki Piarg** (Great Talus), well visible from the hostel and during a walk around Morskie Oko.

## Heading for Czarny Staw (the Black Pond) below Rysy

An under 1h long walk from Morskie Oko along the red trail along a 200 metre rock threshold.

The path to Czarny Staw (The Black Pond) begins on the shoreline of Morskie Oko in the South-eastern direction and turns to the left over a wooden bridge, where Rybi Potok (the Fish Stream) is formed by water spilling over a moraine. The track leads for a time along the lake, through a forest. On your way you will see a small shrine of Matka Boska od Powrotów (Virgin Mary of Safe Returns). We are walking towards the great walls of Mięguszowieckie Szczyty (Mięguszowieckie Summits). The forest ends, dwarf-pines appear. The racket of the hostel slowly dies away. The track splits. To the right leads the path around Morskie Oko, while to the left the trail to Czarny Staw (the Black Pond).

*Mięguszowiecki Szczyt (2438 m asl) is separated from Pośredni Mięguszowiecki Szczyt (Middle Mięguszowiecki Summit – 2393 m asl) by Wyżnia Mięguszowiecka Przełęcz (Upper Mięguszowiecka Pass). In the middle of the picture you can see Kocioł Mięguszowiecki. The green trail to Przełęcz Mięguszowiecka pod Chłopkiem leads along the edge of this dale.*

*Virgin Mary of Safe Returns – the shrine hangs by the path around Morskie Oko, opposite Szczyt Mięguszowiecki (Mięguszowiecki Summit).*

Granite stairs lead along a 200-metre-high rock threshold, which closes Kotlina Czarnego Stawu (The Dale of the Black Pond). From here you can see Morskie Oko with the hostel and a path to Szpiglasowa Przełęcz (Szpiglasowa Pass). A stream of water from Czarny Staw (the Black Pond) falls from a smooth rock, parallel to the path.

We cross the threshold of the upper level of Dolina Rybiego Potoku (The Fish' Stream Valley) and reach Czarny Staw (the Black Pond). We are greeted by an iron cross, made in 1835 in Kuźnice. Silence prevails.

If you are alone here, you should stay for as long as possible. It is really worth it.

**Czarny Staw (the Black Pond) below Rysy** is located at 1581 m asl. Covering the area of 20,5 ha it is one of three largest ponds in Tatra mountains, after Morskie Oko and Wielki Staw (the Great Pond). It is also the second deepest pond, after Wielki Staw in Dolina Pięciu Stawów Polskich (The Valley of Five Polish Ponds).

Czarny Staw (the Black Pond) was created by a glacier. Its water fills a 76,4 metre deep groove within a gigantic granite rock, which threshold closes the dale of Czarny Staw. The sheet of water is 186 metres above

*Black Pond below Rysy.*

*A 200-metre rock threshold separates Morskie Oko from the post-glacier dale filled with the waters of the Black Pond.*

*Czarnostawiańska Siklawa flows from Czarny Staw (the Black Pond) to Morskie Oko along the red trail, connecting both ponds.*

Morskie Oko and it covers a part of the vertical wall of Kazalnica, which rises above Czarny Staw. Although the pond is a poor habitat two types of Cyanophyceae live in its waters.

## Mięguszowiecka Przełęcz pod Chłopkiem (Mięguszowiecka Pass below The Peasant)

A 3 h long walk from Czarny Staw (the Black Pond), through Kocioł Mięguszowiecki (Mięguszowiecki Dale) and Kazalnica, along the green trail.

The green trail leading to Mięguszowiecka Przełęcz pod Chłopkiem (Mięguszowiecka Pass below The Peasant – 2307 m asl) begins just behind the iron cross. The track is not any harder than the high-mountain trails going to Zawrat, Świnica or Rysy.

After walking a certain distance, through a dwarf-mountain-pine forest, we reach a small glade. Beside it, under a large rock, you can find a refuge in mountain rocks called Koleba pod Chłopkiem. In case of a bad weather, several persons can hide here. Mała Siklawa waterfall (Little Siklawa) lays above the refuge. Due to the form of terrain, the trail can be misleading. Yet if you walk slowly, you should not have any problems. In case you loose

*Mięguszowiecka Kazalnica (2159 m asl).*
*The ridge of Czarny Mięguszowiecki Szczyt (Black Mięguszowiecki Summit) falls towards Czarny Staw pod Rysami (the Black Pond below Rysy), along a 500-metre-high precipice. The „Winter" photograph (taken in September) depicts the wall of Kazalnica as seen from the road to Żabi Mnich (Frog's Monk).*

the trail, you should immediately return to the last place, where the trail was present. Shortcuts should not be used in the Tatra mountains.

In less than one hour you should reach the threshold of Kocioł Mięguszowiecki (Mięguszowiecki Dale), which constitutes the base of all three Mięguszowieckie Szczyty (Mięguszowieckie Summits).

**Kocioł Mięguszowiecki (Mięguszowiecki Dale) – Bańdzioch** stretches from the level of 1700 m to 2040 m asl. We walk along a track secured with safety buckles. It leads through the threshold to the upper level of the dale. Inside a small crack in the dale you can still see a small glacier, the remainder of past transformations. Inside Kocioł Mięguszowiecki we can often come across mountain goats and hence silence is worth keeping. After making our way through a rock patch we walk onto Płaśń za Kazalnicą (the Plateau behind Kazalnica) – the top of the wall, that was clearly visible when our journey from Czarny Staw was beginning. We are now at the altitude of 2159 m asl. The trail from Czarny Staw to Kazalnica takes approximately 2 hours to walk.

**Kazalnica Mięguszowiecka** (2159 m asl) is a steep 500-metre-high side ridge of Czarny Mięguszowiecki Szczyt (Black Mięguszowiecki Summit – 2410 m asl), which falls into Czarny Staw below Rysy. Below the sheet of the pond,

*This iron cross was placed on the threshold of Czarny Staw (the Black Pond) in 1836. In the background you can see Morskie Oko in Dolina Rybiego Potoku (the Fish Stream Valley).*

the wall climbs in some places at an angle exceeding 90 degrees. A couple of mountaineer tracks lead through Kazalnica Mieguszowiecka. For example, the extremely difficult track of Łapiński and Paszucha (who crossed it for the first time in 1942), leading ·up the North-eastern wall. The trail leads nearly vertically from the Western shore of Czarny Staw (the Black Pond) along the centreline of the wall. The climb takes around 7 hours in fine weather. The mountaineers are lured by the view of Czarny Staw disappearing beneath them as they struggle up. Their endeavour can be witnessed from the sides of the pond.

A path from Kazalnica leads to the walls of Czarny Mięguszo-

*Czarny Staw pod Rysami (the Black Pond below Rysy)* as seen from the road to Przełęcz Mięguszowiecka (Mięguszowiecka Pass). Frog's lays in the background.

*Dolina Rybiego Potoku (the Fish Stream Valley):* Morskie Oko and Czarny Staw pod Rysami (the Black Pond below Rysy) along with the rock threshold that separates them. You can see the path around Morskie Oko and the hostel.

wiecki Szczyt (Black Mięguszowiecki Summit). A 45 min walk from here, through partially exposed terrain, ends on Mięguszowiecka Przełęcz pod Chłopkiem (Mięguszowiecka Pass below The Peasant). From the pass, in good visibility, you can see the whole track from Bula pod Rysami to the very top of Rysy. Other sights include Dolina Rybiego Potoku (the Fish' Stream Valley), Morskie Oko with the hostel, Czarny Staw (the Black Pond), Żabie (Frog's) and the Slovak High Tatra.

**Mięguszowiecka Przełęcz pod Chłopkiem** (Mięguszowiecka Pass below The Peasant – 2307 m asl) is located between two peaks of Mięguszowieckie Szczyty (Mięguszowieckie Summits), Czarny Szczyt (Black Summit – 2410 m asl) and Pośredni Szczyt (Middle Summit – 2393 m asl). It is a wide, shaded pass. It owes its name to the dark crag of Chłopek, which rises on the left. You should bow politely to the mountain, or else...

The pass lies on the border. Below you can see Dolina Mięguszowiecka (Mięguszowiecka Valley) with the largest pond on the Slovak side, Wielki Staw Hińczowy (The Great Hińczowy Pond). Lets take a short look at the valley and the pond.

*Dolina Rybiego Potoku (the Fish' Stream Valley) with the massif of Opalone (on the left), which separates it from Dolina Roztoki. In the background you can see Wołoszyn.*

*Other photos: On the peak of **Kazalnica**, Żabi Szczyt (Frog's Summit) and the ridge of Żabi (Frog's) visible in the background.*

### Kocioł Mięguszowiecki (Mięguszowiecki Dale) – Mięguszowiecki Bańdzioch

The dale between Czarny Szczyt Mięguszowiecki and Mięguszowiecki Szczyt at the foot of Pośredni Szczyt Mięguszowiecki. Climate conditions allow a small glacier to remain on the bottom of the dale. During the Winter large amounts of snow and ice gather here. This causes a constant avalanche threat. In the dale you can sometimes find mountain goats looking for peace and quiet (upper photo). The picture on the bottom depicts the upper part of Kazalnica precipices. In the middle, you can see mountaineers resting after a completed climbout.

**Wielki Staw Hińczowy** (the Great Hińczowy Pond) is located at the altitude of 1946 m asl. Covering an area of 20 ha it is the fourth largest pond in Tatra mountains. It is 53 m deep, placing it on the third place in the ranking. Mały Staw Hińczowy (Small Hińczowy Pond), 6,4 metre deep and covering an area of 2,2 ha lays below the pond, at the altitude of 1923 m asl. Both ponds are part of **Mięguszowiecka Dolina** (Mięguszowiecka Valley), one of the largest valleys in the Slovak Tatra. The valley is closed from the West by Grań Baszt (The Crag of Towers), with its highest peaks of Szatan (Satan – 2416 m asl) and Koprowy Szczyt (Koprowy Summit – 2363 m asl). In the North the valley ends by the border summits of Cubryna through Mięguszowieckie Szczyty and Wołowy Grzbiet (Ox's Rib) all the way to Rysy, joined from the East with Wysoka and Popradzka Kopa (Popradzka Pile – 2354 m asl) via a ridge.

Hińczowy Potok (the Hińczowy Stream) originates in Wielki Staw Hińczowy and, in the middle part of Mięguszowiecka Dolina, converges with Żabi Potok (the Frog's Stream) flowing from Mały Żabi Staw Mięguszowiecki (The Small Mięguszowiecki Frog's Pond). The joined waters of these two streams form Potok Mięguszowiecki (Mięguszowiecki Stream). This stream in turn flows into Krupa, a stream flowing from Popradzki Staw, creating **Poprad**, which later, already in Poland, joins Dunajec.

*Przełęcz Mięguszowiecka pod Chłopkiem (Mięguszowiecka Pass below The Peasant – 2307 m asl) that separates Pośredni Szczyt Mięguszowiecki (Middle Mięguszowiecki Summit) from Czarny Szczyt Mięguszowiecki (Black Mięguszowiecki Summit).*

# Rysy

A 4 hour long excursion from Morskie Oko along the red trail through Czarny Staw (the Black Pond), Bula, Kocioł pod Reglami (Dale below the Bolts) to the North-western peak of Rysy.

The route to Rysy starts near Morskie Oko and initially goes along the path running around the lake and further to Czarny Staw (the Black Pond).

By Czarny Staw, besides the iron cross, where the green trail heads towards Mięguszowiecka Przełęcz, the red trail turns left and leads around the pond, crossing a stream flowing from a rock threshold down to Morskie Oko. The walls of Żabi (Frog's) overlook the path, while on the opposite side we can clearly see the great wall of Kazalnica. It will keep us company throughout our journey.

We are on the South-eastern shore of Czarny Staw (the Black Pond). The trail leads along a zigzag path towards a threshold of a pile of rocks rising above, created by stones rolling down from Wołowy Szczyt (Ox's Summit) and especially from Żabia Przełęcz (Frog's Pass – 2225 m asl). Moving on, we cross other rock thresholds, which crave the slope. In this terrain, even in late Spring you can find large fields of snow. We are now in a rock gully. After crossing it, we will begin our climb to **Bula pod**

*Wielki Staw Hińczowy (the Great Hińczowy Pond) and Mały Staw Hińczowy (the Little Hińczowy Pond) in Dolina Mięguszowiecka (Mięguszowiecka Valley) on the Slovak side.*

**Rysami** (2054 m asl). The rocky monticule closes Kocioł pod Rysami (The Dale below Rysy) from the North.

We are on the upper level of Dolina Rybiego Potoku (the Fish Stream Valley), which crosses three post-glacier dales: Kocioł Morskiego Oka (The Dale of Morskie Oko) with its moraine, Kocioł Czarnego Stawu (The Dale of the Blach Pond) with its rock threshold, and Kocioł pod Rysami (The Dale below Rysy) with the rocky monticule.

**Kocioł pod Rysami** is surrounded by 400 metre-high walls of Wyżni Żabi Szczyt (Upper Frog's Summit – 2259 m asl), well visible Niżnie Rysy (Lower Rysy – 2430 m asl) with Rysy (2499 m asl) and Wołowy Grzbiet (Ox's Rib). The track from Czarny Staw (the Black Pond) to Kocioł pod Rysami takes over one hour to walk.

We are now facing a climb through carved ledges with the aid of chains and buckles. As we reach higher altitudes the view at the valley beneath becomes wider. Before we begin the final climb, we can take a longer look at a horizontal crack in the rocky base of the summit. This rift depicts the scale of the stretching and squeezing forces, which shaped granite, when the Tatra were being created. The trail leads right besides this great rift,

*Rysy (2499 m asl).*
  *The highest Polish peak is fenced off from Niżnie Rysy (Lower Rysy – 2430 m asl) by Przełęcz pod Rysami (the Pass below Rysy). On the right, in the distance, already on the Slovak side lays Wysoka (Tall – 2560 m asl).*

where the snow lays long. It turns towards the Eastern side of Rysy and runs above the Slovak Ciężka Dolina (Difficult Valley). Beneath us, two hectares of Zmarzły Staw (the Frozen Pond – 1760 m asl), which is located by the Northern wall of Wysoka (Tall – 2547 m asl) and the crag of Galeria Gankowa (Porch Gallery).

The North-western peak of Rysy is right in front of us. We are at 2499 m asl, on the highest summit in Poland. If you reach this place, you will surely meet a handful of tourists from various countries.

**Rysy (2503 m asl)** towers above three valleys: Dolina Rybiego Potoku (Fish' Stream Valley) on the Polish side and two Slovak valleys – Dolina Mięguszowiecka (Mięguszowiecka Valley) and Dolina Białej Wody (White Water Valley). The mountain is also a junction point of three ridges. The main ridge of Tatra ranges to the West, to Liliowe (Made of Lilies), Świnica and further to Mięguszowieckie Szczyty (Mięguszowieckie Summits). The second ridge heads South-east, to the highest summit of Tatra mountains, **Gierlach** (2654 m asl) through Wysoka (Tall), Ganek (Porch). The third ridge leads North, through Niżnie Rysy (Lower Rysy) onto Żabie (Frog). The massif of Rysy lays between three passes. The first one is Żabia Przełęcz (Frog's Pass – 2225 m asl) which separates Rysy from Żabi Koń

*North-western peak of Rysy (2499 m asl).*
*Some say that this was Lenin. Maybe its true, the plate visible on the photograph certainly was here at some point, but hasn't been seen by anyone for years...*

(Frog's Horse – 2291 m asl) and Wołowy Grzbiet (Ox's Rib). The second pass is Przełęcz pod Rysami (The Pass below Rysy – 2365 m asl) which divides Rysy from Niżnie Rysy (2430 m asl). The third pass is Waga (The Scale – 2340 m asl) with the peak of Wysoka (Tall – 2547 m asl) laying behind it.

The Summit of Rysy comprises of three peaks: the highest is the one in the middle (2503 m asl), the North-western one (2499 m asl) and the lowest, South-eastern one (2473 m asl).

During the Summer you can cross the border on Rysy and visit the Slovak side. You can walk along the red trail, which leads down a very

*Mięguszowieckie Summits* as seen from the track to Rysy.

*A view at the Slovak side from Rysy: Młynarz (The Miller – 2170 m asl) above Dolina Białej Wody (White Water Valley) is on the foreground. In the background you can see Bielskie Tatra mountains with Hawrań (2154 m asl).*

*A view of Polish High Tatra from Rysy.* On the foreground of the upper photo you can see Miedziane (Copper – 2233 m asl) with Opalony Wierch (2115 m asl). Between them lays the wide Przełęcz Marchwiczna (Carrot Pass – 2055 m asl), from which gullies fall towards Morskie Oko (avalanches during the Winter). In the background you see the ridge above Dolina Pięciu Stawów Polskich (The Valley of Five Polish Ponds) from Kozi Wierch (Goat's Wierch – 2291 m asl), through Granaty, Wielka Buczynowa Turnia (Great Beech Crag – 2184 m asl) above Dolina Buczynowa (Beech Valley), to Krzyżne and Wielki Wołoszyn (2155 m asl). In the foreground of the bottom picture is Szpiglasowy Wierch (2172 m asl) and the mountain path leading to Przełęcz Szpiglasowa (Szpiglasowa Pass – 2110 m asl). In the background lays świnica with the ridge to Kasprowy Wierch (1987 m asl) and Western Tatra.

*A view at High Tatra from Rysy:* Upper photo: Lodowy Szczyt (Ice Summit – 2627 m asl), Durny Szczyt (Dumb Summit – 2623 m asl), Łomnica (2634 m asl), Mały Lodowy (Small Ice – 2461 m asl), Pośrednia Grań (Middle Ridge – 2440 m asl), Mała Wysoka (Little Tall – 2428 m asl), Staroleśny Szczyt (Old-forest Summit – 2452 m asl), Litworowy Szczyt (Litworowy Summit – 2423 m asl), the massif of **Gierlach** with Zadni (Rear – 2638 m asl) – the highest summit in the whole Tatra.

On the right, in the shade, lays the North-western wall of Galeria Gankowa (Porch Gallery) in the massif of Ganek (The Porch – 2459 m asl).

***Frog's Ridge.*** *It separates Dolina Rybiego Potoku (the Fish' Stream Valley) from Białczańska Żabia Dolina (Białczan Frog's Valley) on the Slovak side. The ponds visible on the upper photo are Białczańskie Żabie Stawy (Białczan Frog's Ponds) – the Upper and the Lower. Żabi Potok (the Frog's Stream) originates in these ponds. The massif on the right is Młynarz (The Miller –* *2170 m asl), which closes the valley and is connected via a ridge with Wyżni Żabi Szczyt (Upper Frog's Summit – 2259 m asl). Młynarz keeps us company all the way to Morskie Oko.*

*The lower photo depicts the other side of Żabia Przełęcz (Frog's Ridge) with Apostoły (The Apostles), row of crags, well visible from the track to Rysy.*

easy path to a hostel below Waga called **Chata pod Rysami** (The Cottage below Rysy) built at the altitude of 2255 m asl. Further on, the trail leads down Mięguszowiecka Dolina to Popradzki Staw (the Popradzki Pond). After 15 minutes of walking along the yellow trail from Popradzki Staw you should reach the feet of the Western slope of Osterwa (1984 m asl). A symbolic monument in the memory of those, who died in the mountains stands here.

The way down from Rysy to the hostel by Morskie Oko, along the same path as we went up, should take around 3 hours. This way we complete our high-mountain excursions in the Southern part of the valley of Rybi Potok (the Fish Stream). We will now move to the Western side, towards Mnich (The Monk), Wrota Chałubińskiego (Chałubiński's Doors), Szpiglasowy Wierch with Szpiglasowa Przełęcz and Miedziane (Copper) with Świstówka.

## Wrota Chałubińskiego (Chałubiński's Doors)
A 2-hour-30-minute-long walk from Morskie Oko, along the red and yellow trails through gullies, Dolina za Mnichem (The Valley behind The Monk) to Wrota Chałubińskiego (Chałubiński's Doors).

The trail begins opposite to the old hostel by Morskie Oko and in its first part leads along the path to Szpiglasowa Przełęcz (Szpiglasowa Pass). It is a wide granite track, which traverses the sides of Miedziany (Copper) among dwarf-mountain-pines. The traverse curves widely making the walk effortless.

The part of the path above the Western shore of Morskie Oko crosses avalanche-gullies (called: Marchwiczny (Carrot-like), Urwany (Ripped-out) and Szeroki (Wide)), which create piles of rocks reaching down to Morskie Oko. Further on, the trail reaches a porch of a small valley called Dolinka pod Spadami (The Valley below Slopes), which lays below Kocioł Mnichowy (Monk's Dale). Żleb pod Mnichem (Gully below the Monk) along with its

*The view from Morskie Oko in the South-western direction. On the upper picture, on the left, you can see the ridge of Cubryna, the crag of Mniszek (2045 m asl), Mnich (The Monk – 2070 m asl, the South-western wall –mountaineer's „R" variant), Liptowskie Mury (Liptowskie Walls) with Wrota Chałubińskiego* (Chałubiński's Doors – 2022 m asl) heading in Szpiglasowy Wierch direction. The wall of Miedziane (Copper) closes the encirclement. The second photo depicts a part of yellow trail to Szpiglasowa Przełęcz (Szpiglasowa Pass) and Wrota Chałubińskiego (which turns red by the threshold of Dolina za Mnichem).

Eastern wall can be seen above. Below lays Dwoista Siklawa (two waterfalls, Prosty (The Straight One) and Skośny (The Skewed One) are well visible from the path around the lake). Its waters fall into Morskie Oko.

After 1h 30min we reach the edge of **Dolina za Mnichem** (The Valley behind the Monk). The yellow trail leads from here to Szpiglasowa Przełęcz (Szpiglasowa Pass). The red trail, which appears here, will take us to Wrota Chałubińskiego (Chałubiński's Doors) in one hour.

**Dolina za Mnichem** (The Valley behind the Monk: 1785 m asl – 2100 m asl) constitutes the upper level of Dolina Rybiego Potoku (the Fish Stream Valley). It is surrounded by ridges stretching from Miedziane and Szpiglasowy Wierch to the South-west towards Ciemnosmreczyńska Turnia (Dark-pine Crag), Zadni Mnich (Rear Monk) and Cubryna along with Mnich (the Monk) in the main ridge of Tatra. There are few ponds in this tiny, one-kilometre-long valley. Staw Staszica (the Staszic's Pond – upper and lower – 1785 m asl) is located on the bottom of the valley. Depending on the intensity of rainfalls and the water level, this pond can comprise of two or more smaller interconnected ponds.

There are several small seasonal ponds below Mnich (the Monk). These are Wyżnie Mnichowe Stawki (the Upper Monk's Ponds). While the tiny Zadni Mnichowy Stawek (The Rear Monk's Pond) lays below Cubryna, at the altitude of 2070 m asl. Its water sheet can be covered with ice and snow even till late

*Wrota Chałubińskiego (Chałubiński's Doors – 2022 m asl, Ciemnosmreczyńska Turnia on the left )*
*as seen from Staw Staszica (the Staszic's Pond).*

**Mnich** (The Monk – 2070 m asl) – its sharp crag is one of the most recognisable summits in the neighbourhood of Morskie Oko. It comprises of two peaks – the South-eastern one and the shorter, South-western one. The two peaks are connected by a short ridge with Mniszek (Little Monk – 2045 m asl) – an adjacent crag well visible from Morskie Oko. Mnich lays in the main ridge of Tatra mountains. Popular mountaineer trails lead along its walls. Wyżnie Mnichowe Stawki (the Upper Monk's Ponds) lay on the Western side of the summit. The lower photo shows Dolinka za Mnichem (Valley behind the Monk) with the double Staw Staszica.

Summer. The altitude at which the pond lays makes it the highest located pond in Tatra mountains.

Stawek na Kopkach (The Pond on Piles) closes the gallery of ponds of Dolina za Mnichem.

The valley owes its name to the sharp and well visible from Morskie Oko crag of **Mnich** (The Monk – 2070 m asl, the crag besides Mnich is called Mniszek – Little Monk). The crag will keep us company throughout this excursion. Along the Eastern side of Mnich lead numerous famous mountaineers' tracks including Wariant R (Variant R).

A similar crag of Zadni Mnich (Rear Monk – 2172 m asl) is located above the main crag.

After passing Staw Staszica (the Staszic's Pond) we reach a rocky, narrowing gully. The trail leads further up, through steep zigzags, to **Wrota Chałubińskiego** (Chałubiński's Doors) at the altitude of 2022 m asl. This landmark is practically a narrow valley between Kopa nad Wrotami (The Pile above the Doors – 2075 m asl) and the ridge of Szpiglasowy Wierch.

On the other side you can see the ponds in Ciemnosmreczyńska Dolina (Dark-pine Valley) in the Slovak Republic.

*The red trail to* **Wrota Chałubińskiego** *(Chałubiński's Doors – 2022 m asl): A field of snow in the middle of Summer in the Dolina za Mnichem (Valley behind the Monk – photo on the right)* • *The final parts of the track; a view of Mnich and the surroundings of Morskie Oko (upper photo)* • *The yellow trail to Szpiglasowa Przełęcz (2110 m asl – bottom picture).*

**Wrota Chałubińskiego** *(2022 m asl) – Dolina za Mnichem is visible in the distance along with Staw Staszica. The red trail to Wrota Chałubińskiego leads through the valley. Wrota Chałubińskiego is a pass between Kopa nad Wrotami (The Pile above the Doors – 2075 m asl) and Szpiglasowy Wierch (2172 m asl). It lays in the main ridge of Tatra mountains. On the left you* can see the zigzags of the track to Szpiglasowa Przełęcz.

*The bottom picture depicts the Slovak Ciemnosmreczyński Wyżni Staw (Dark-pine Upper Pond) in Piarżysta Dolina (Scree Valley). In the future Wrota Chałubińkiego will constitute a very convenient connection between Morskie Oko and Dolina Koprowa (Koprowa Valley).*

## Szpiglasowa Przełęcz (Szpiglasowa Pass)

A 2-hour-30-minute-long walk from Morskie Oko along the yellow trail, through Dolina za Mnichem (The Valley behind the Monk) to Szpiglasowa Przełęcz. The track to Dolina za Mnichem is the same one which leads to Wrota Chałubińskiego (Chałubiński's Doors).

Szpiglasowa Przełęcz is an important pass as it connects Dolina Rybiego Potoku (The Valley of Fish Stream) with Dolina Pięciu Stawów Polskich (The Valley of Five Polish Ponds) and further, through Zawrat or Kozią Przełęcz (The Goat's Pass), with Dolina Gąsienicowa (GąsieniceValley).

From the threshold of Dolina za Mnichem (The Valley behind the Monk) the yellow trail continues its traverse of Miedziane (Copper) and finally reaches the narrow Tatra mountain path. From here you can marvel at the beautiful sights of Morskie Oko and Czarny Staw. The path leads to Szpiglasowa Przełęcz (2110 m asl), which lays between Szpiglasowy Wierch (2172 m asl) and Miedziane (2233 m asl). The pass till late Spring and early in Autumn can be covered with snow. The crossing from the pass to Dolina Pięciu Stawów (The Valley of Five Polish Ponds) is a steep gully secured with chains and buckles.

*The upper parts of the mountain path to **Szpiglasowa Przełęcz** (Szpiglasowa Pass – 2110 m asl, yellow trail). The path connects Dolina Rybiego Potoku (the Fish's Stream Valley) with Dolina Pięciu Stawów Polskich (The Valley of Five Polish Ponds).*

## Świstówka Roztocka

A 2 hour long walk from Morskie Oko along the blue trail, through Świstówka, Świstowa Czuba to Przedni Staw Polski (The Frontal Polish Pond).

This track is an alternative route from Dolina Rybiego Potoku (Fish' Stream Valley) to Dolina Pięciu Stawów Polskich (The Valley of Five Polish Ponds). You can also take the path through Szpiglasowa Przełęcz (Szpiglasowa Pass). The choice between the two options should be based on where you want to go to from Dolina Pięciu Stawów.

The blue trail begins on a road by Morskie Oko opposite a group of small ponds. It leads into a spruce forest.

After crossing Głęboki Żleb (Deep Gully), we reach the summit of Kępa (1683 m asl – a sight-spot for the High Tatra), covered with rocks. As we climb up (watch out for mountain goats), we enter a small rocky valley called Świstówka Roztocka in the upper part of Dolina Roztoki (Roztoka Valley).

Further on we walk towards the precipice of Opalone ridge, which culminates at Świstowa Czuba (1763 m asl) with 300-metre-deep precipices into Dolina Roztoki. Then we head to a small pass below Świstowa Czuba, from where our path turns and leads down to the hostel by Przedni Staw (the Frontal Pond).

When walking along this track, leading above three valleys, one can get an idea about the size of Dolina Białki and the proportions of its multiple levels.

*The blue trail from Morskie Oko, through Świstówka, to Przedni Staw Polski (the Frontal Polish Pond). An alternative connection between Dolina Rybiego Stawu (the Fish' Stream Valley) and Dolina Pięciu Stawów Polskich (The Valley of Five Polish Ponds).*

# Dolina Pięciu Stawów Polskich (The Valley of Five Polish Ponds)

Since Dolina Pięciu Stawów Polskich is a post-glacier lower level of Dolina Roztoki (Roztoka Valley) it can be perceived as the third branch of the vast Dolina Białki (Białka Valley). There are no paved roads here, no car-parks only mountains surrounding the lakes. Nature has created this valley over 85 m above the lower level of Wielka Siklawa waterfall on Stawiarska Ściana (Stawiarska Wall) and almost one kilometre above Kuźnice.

Szpiglasowy Wierch, which lays on the South side, is a junction point of ridges stretching in two directions. To the South-east, the ridge of Miedziane (Copper) and Opalony Wierch, rises 560 metres above the lakes. The ridges of Liptowskie Mury (Liptowskie Walls), Kotelnica together with Gładki (Smooth) and Walentkowy Wierch range to the North-west.

Almost 400 metre high walls overlook the valley from the North. They rise above the upper level of the valley, creating the crag of Świnica leading to Kozi Wierch, which in turn rises 626 metres above Wielki Staw. Also from the North the side crag of Kołowa Czuba intersects the valley creating Dolinka pod Kołem (The Valley under a Wheel) in the West and Dolinka Pusta (Empty Valley) in the East.

A granite threshold separates Dolina Pięciu Stawów (The Valley of Five Polish Ponds) from Dolina Roztoki (Roztoka Valley).

The giant rock between the two valleys is not the only thing, which sets them apart. Dolina Roztoki, tucked between Wołoszyn and Opalone and covered with old spruce and stone-pine trees, was created by a receding glacier. Yet its building potential here was

*Opalony Wierch (2115 m asl) above Przedni Staw Polski (the Frontal Polish Pond). Wielki Staw (the Great Pond) is on the right. Above is the ridge from Przełęcz Marchwiczna (Carrot Pass – 2055 m asl) that leads to Miedziane (Copper). The blue trail from Morskie Oko runs along the left side of Opalone through Świstowa Czuba (1763 m asl).*

much weaker than in Dolina Pięciu Stawów. The latter is the largest post-glacier lake in Tatra. It lays among grass, rocks and dwarf mountain pines and is a genuine 61 ha masterpiece.

Let us take a closer look at these lakes, classifying them according to the altitude they are at.

## Wielki Staw Polski (The Great Polish Pond)

Wielki Staw Polski is located at 1665 m asl and is the lowest-located pond in the group. The water from all the other ponds flows into Wielki Staw Polski spills over a rock threshold, creating a stream which quickly turns into a large waterfall and finally Potok Roztoki (the Roztoki Stream). The pond has the largest capacity of all ponds in Tatra. It is also the deepest, up to 79,3 m of depth, and the longest, stretching for almost 2 km. It is as long as the whole Dolina za Mnichem (the Valley behind the Monk). The area of Wielki Staw Polski, 34 ha, is comparable to that of Morskie Oko.

## Mały Staw Polski (The Small Polish Pond)

Mały Staw Polski is located at 1668 m asl, between Wielki Staw Polski and Przedni Staw Polski (the Frontal Polish Pond). It is really a small pond, covering mere 0,18 ha and only 2,1 m deep. The small difference of altitudes between Mały Staw Polski, Wielki Staw Polski and Przedni Staw Polski lay – 1 to 4 metres – leads to merging of these three ponds during large rainfalls or Spring thaws. Initially the Small Pond joins with the Great Pond and later the two fuse with the Frontal Pond and create one fantastic lake.

## Przedni Staw Polski (the Frontal Polish Pond)

This pond is located at 1669 m asl, on the Eastern side of Wielka Siklawa and can be clearly seen, when walking along Orla Perć (Eagle's Mountain Path) above Dolinka Buczynowa (Beech Valley). It covers 7,72 ha, and is 34,6 metres deep.

The Frontal Pond is the first pond of the group that we come across, when walking from Dolina Rybiego Potoku (the Fish' Stream Valley) along the blue trail through świstówka Roztocka. There is a hostel by this pond. It is supplied from the upper part of Dolina Roztoki (Roztoka Valley). The hostel is worth recommending especially after the tourist season to anyone who longs for peace and loneliness.

## Czarny Staw Polski (The Black Polish Pond)

Czarny Staw Polski is located at 1722 m asl right under the slope of Kotelnica. It covers 12,65 ha and its greatest depth is 50,4 m. It lays on the left from the yellow trail leading from Morskie Oko through Szpiglasowa Przełęcz and is divided from the Great Pond by a rock threshold.

Czarny Staw Polski (The Black Polish Pond) is very well visible from Dolinka Pusta (Empty Valley) as it closes the valley from the South.

## Wole Oko (Ox's Eye)

Wole Oko (without „Polish" this time) is located below Zadni Staw Polski (the Rear Polish Pond) at 1867 m asl. Its covers less than 0,1 ha.

The pond owes its existence to the Rear Pond, the waters of which when flowing towards the Great Pond, fill the niche of Wole Oko. The pond freezes during the Winter just like the Small Pond. In terms of its name it is not counted as one of the ponds of Dolina Pięciu Stawów Polskich (The Valley of Five Polish Ponds).

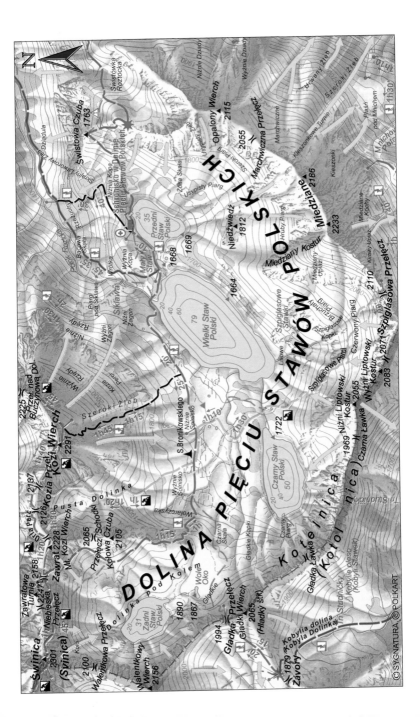

### Zadni Staw Polski (the Rear Polish Pond)

Zadni Staw Polski lays by a threshold of Dolinka pod Kołem (the Valley below the Wheel), at the feet of Walentkowy Wierch at 1890 m asl. It covers 6,64 ha and is 31,6 m deep. The highest-located pond in Polish Tatra is the tiny (0,04 ha) Zadni Mnichowy Stawek (the Rear Monk's Pond) in Dolina za Mnichem (The Valley behind The Monk), which lays at 2070 m asl. Zadni Staw takes the second place in this discipline.

Zadni Staw can be seen in all its glory from the path to Świnica on the side of Zawrat.

### Along the valley between the lakes

We recommend this track especially to those who stay at the hostel by Przedni Staw. The trail leads initially along the shores of Frontal, Small and Great Polish Pond and then into the upper levels of the valley.

*The yellow trail leads from **Krzyżne** to Dolina Pięciu Stawów Polskich (The Valley of Five Polish Ponds), through the threshold of Dolinka Buczynowa (Beech Valley).*

*__Krzyżne (2112 m asl)__ – a junction pass of three ridges: from Wielki Wołoszyn (2155 m asl), from Wielka Koszysta (2193 m asl) above Dolina Pańszczyca, and from Wielka Buczynowa Turnia (2184 m asl).*

## Szpiglasowa Przełęcz (Szpiglasowa Pass)

A 1 hour 30 minutes long walk from Niżnie Solnisko along the yellow trail, through Szpiglasowy Kocioł (Szpiglasowy Dale) to Szpiglasowa Pass.

We enter the yellow trail on Niżnie Solnisko, where it branches off from the blue trail, leading southwards to Zawrat. The path is called Szpiglasowa Perć (the Mountain Path of Szpiglasowa).

Niżnie Solnisko is a place in the lower part of Dolina Pięciu Stawów Polskich (the Valley of Five Polish Ponds), where once cubes of salt were set out for sheep. This was a standard custom in the times when Spring and Autumn shepherding was a normal practice in these areas. But now its history.

From Niżnie Solnisko the trail leads between Czarny Staw (the Black Pond) and Wielki Staw (the Great Pond), along a moraine which separates them. On the left, above Wielki Staw but below the rock threshold, you will find four small Szpiglasowe Stawki (the Szpiglasowe Ponds). The path leads below the slope of Niżni Liptowski Kostur (2055 m asl) towards the lower edge of **Kocioł Szpiglasowy**. We are on Czerwony Piarg (Red Scree) a rocky scree-covered area, which when covered with snow turns into a steep snow-field – a peculiar tourist attraction especially in Spring.

Szpiglasowa Perć leads towards a long gully. After forcing it, with help of buckles etc., we reach Szpiglasowa Przełęcz. Further on, the track runs down to Morskie Oko (under 2 h 30 min) omitting Miedziane (Copper) – a strict nature preserve. The way back to Wielki Staw Polski (the Great Polish Pond) leads along the same route.

*Two opposing slopes surrounding **Dolina Pięciu Stawów Polskich** (The Valley of Five Polish Ponds). One belongs to Świnica (2301 m asl – the photo on the left), while the other to Szpiglasowy Wierch (2172 m asl – photo on the right).*

The tourist hostel in Dolina Pięciu Stawów Polskich above Przedni Staw.

Dolina Pięciu Stawów Polskich: the stream that flows from Wielki Staw towards Wielka Siklawa gives rise to Potok Roztoki.

Wielki Staw Polski and Przedni Staw. On the right are the slopes of Miedziane.

**Morskie Oko**

A 2-hour-long walk from Świstowa Czuba, along the blue trail, through Świstówka Roztocka and Kępa.

An effortless and at the same time the fastest connection between Dolina Pięciu Stawów Polskich (The Valley of Five Polish Ponds) and Morskie Oko begins near the hostel by Przedni Staw (the Frontal Pond). It leads from its Northern shore through rocky terrain and dwarf-mountain-pines to Świstowa Czuba (1763 m asl). The path is carved on its side by a not very visible, but almost vertical, 300 metre deep precipice falling into Dolina Roztoki. The Eastern ridge of Orla Perć (Eagle's Mountain Path) with Dolinka Buczynowa (Beech Valley) and the path to Krzyżne form a wonderful sight when looking to the North from the trail. If you are planning to walk to Dolina Gąsienicowa (Gąsienice Valley) through Krzyżne, you may want to take a look at the yellow trail, which leads there. The path heads North towards **Świstówka Roztocka**, a small valley in the upper level of Dolina Roztoki. It is littered with rocks covered with moss. After crossing the valley we reach a meadow called Wolarnia, a used-to-be sheep-run placed on the slope of **Kępa**. Further on, the trail leads through a forest, along the slopes of Opalony Wierch, above a well visible road from Włosienica. Our path joins the road and the red trail running along it to Morskie Oko.

**Krzyżne**

A 2 hour walk from Wielki Staw (the Great Pond) along the yellow trail, through Buczynowa Dolinka and Żleb pod Krzyżnem (the Gully below Krzyżne).

Our trip starts at a junction of trails near a bridge above the stream from Wielki Staw (the Great Pond) to Wielka Siklawa (Great Siklawa). The yellow trail separates from the

*Szpiglasowa Przełęcz (Szpiglasowa Pass – 2110 m asl) as seen from Dolina Pięciu Stawów Polskich (The Valley of Five Polish Ponds). Below, the yellow trail traverses towards Czarny Staw Polski (the Black Polish Pond) and Wielki Staw Polski (the Great Polish Pond).*

blue trail, which leads along the valley to Zawrat. As we walk from the hostel by Przedni Staw (the Frontal Pond) we cross a green trail, running down Dolina Roztoki (Roztoka Valley) to Wodogrzmoty Mickiewicza (Mickiewicz' Waterfalls – approx. 2h)

In the lower part we traverse a long slope of Kozi Wierch (Goat's Wierch), walking through dwarf-mountain-pines and large blocks of rocks. We head North and reach the rocky Dolinka Buczynowa (Beech Valley). Then along the edge of the bottom of a dale hanging from the Eastern ridge of Orla Perć (Eagle's Path).

### Dolinka Buczynowa (Beech Valley)

Dolinka Buczynowa is a classic example of a hanging valley. This type of valleys is common in Tatra. It hangs at 1700-1950 m asl forming the upper branch of Dolina Roztoki (Roztoka Valley), falling into it with a granite threshold. This 1km-long post-glacier dale is surrounded by the slopes of Kozi Wierch (Goat's Wierch), ridges of Granaty (Granates) and Buczynowe Turnie (Beech Crags). The valley is laden with stones and scree. Buczynowa Siklawa flows from under the ridge closing the valley into Potok Roztoki (the Roztoka Stream).

The path leads along a steep, grassy side of Mała Buczynowa Turnia (Little Beech Crag) and through a record high 700-metre-long Żleb pod Krzyżnem (Gully below Krzyżne), which ends with a smooth path. The last traverse. **Krzyżne** lays in front of us. We are at 2112 m asl in the junction point of three great ridges: Grań Wielkiego Wołoszyna (The Ridge of Great Wołoszyn – 2155 m asl), Grań Wielkiej Koszystej (The Ridge of Great Koszysta – 2193 m asl) and Grań Wielkiej Buczynowej Turni (The Ridge of Great Beech Crag – 2184 m asl).

The path has no climbing sections because Krzyżne lays between two valleys, Dolina Pańszczycy (Pańszczyca Valley) and Dolina Roztoki (Roztoka Valley), and is just a link between them. The remaining three trails which lead through Kozi Wierch (Goat's Wierch), Kozia Przełęcz (Goat's Pass) and Zawrat require some climbing. The yellow trail

*A shack in the middle of Dolina Pięciu Stawów Polskich.*

From Krzyżne leads through Dolina Pańszczycy to Murowaniec in Dolina Gąsienicowa (Gąsienice Valley). It is a pleasant, effortless, 2-hour-long walk.

### Kozi Wierch (Goat's Wierch)
A 1-hour-45-minute-long walk from Wielki Staw (the Great Polish Pond) along the black trail through Szeroki Żleb (Wide Gully) to Kozi Wierch.

The trail begins by Wielki Staw Polski, where it branches off to the North from the blue trail going to Zawrat. We climb a steep southern wall of Kozi Wierch and make our way through Szeroki Żleb (Wide Gully) coming down from the mountain. In the upper part we come across a rocky traverse, which leads to the right towards the red trail. The trail leads to Orla Perć. From here we walk along another rocky traverse and finally reach the summit of Kozi Wierch – 2291 m asl.

### Kozi Wierch
Kozi Wierch (Goat's Wierch – 2291 m asl) is the highest summit, which lays entirely on the Polish territory. It overlooks Dolina Pięciu Stawów Polskich (The Valley of Five Polish Ponds) and Kozia Dolinka (Goat's Valley), which constitute the upper part of Dolina Gąsienicowa (Gąsienice Valley). It does not lay in the main ridge of Tatra, but rather in the side ridge, that links Świnica with the massif of Wołoszyn. It is the culmination point of Kozie Wierchy, between Mały Kozi Wierch (Little Goat's Wierch) and the ridge of Czarne Ściany (Black Walls). All its sides are steep except the Southern slope, which is relatively easy. We climbed along this side of Kozi Wierch, when heading for Wielki Staw (Great Pond).

The easiest way from Kozi Wierch to Dolina Gąsienicowa (Gąsienice Valley) leads through Orla Perć (Eagle's Mountain Path) to the black trail (45 min to Żleb

*Kozi Wierch (2291 m asl) – the tallest Polish summit, that lays entirely on the Polish side. On the left you can see the wall of Zamarła Turnia. The black trail leads from Wielki Staw (the Great Pond) to Kozi Wierch.*

Kulczyńskiego (Kulczyński's Gully)), and along this trail to Zmarzły Staw (the Frozen Pond) and further to Murowaniec. The red trail heads in the opposite direction, to Kozia Przełęcz (Goat's Pass – 1 h 40 min with climbing) and then down to Zmarzły Staw.

## Kozia Przełęcz (Goat's Pass)
A 1-hour-30-minute-long walk from Wyżnie Solnisko along the yellow trail, through Dolinka Pusta (Empty Valley) to Kozia Przełęcz.

The trail begins below Czarny Staw (the Black Pond), on Wyżnie Solnisko, beside a large block of stone with Tablica Bronikowskiego (Bronikowski's Plate). Here the yellow trail branches off to the North from the blue trail. The whole track runs through crevasses in large blocks of rock. Initially we climb onto a rocky ridge with huge boulders. This is the Southern boundary of the post-glacier hanging valley called **Dolinka Pusta** (Empty Valley), which lays on the upper level of Dolina Pięciu Stawów (The Valley of Five Polish Ponds). The side ridge of Kołowa Czuba running from Mały Kozi Wierch (Little Goat's Wierch) sliced the main valley in two, creating Dolinka Pusta and Dolina pod Kołem (Valley under the Wheel). The moraine of Czarny Staw, laying to the South, is also worth taking a closer look at. We can see it clearly as we climb up the steep wall of Kozi Wierch. After making our way through a scree-covered terrain we reach a vast gully between Kozie Czuby and the southern wall of Zamarła Turnia, which closes the valley from the North. From here the trail leads through the edge of the gully, along the walls of Kozie Czuby. Some climbing is necessary. Using chains and buckles we make our way to the top of **Kozia Przełęcz** (Goat's Pass – 2137 m asl).

*A view from Zawrat:* In the foreground – Kołowa Czuba, further – Opalony Wierch, Miedziane (Copper) and Szpiglasowy Wierch, in the background – (from the left) Świstowy Szczyt (Świstowy Summit – 2383 m asl), Slawkowski (2453 m asl), the massif of Gierlach (2654 m asl), Rysy (2499 m asl), Wysoka (2560 m asl), Kończysta (2540 m asl), Mięguszowiecki Szczyt (2436 m asl), Cubryna (2376 m asl) and Koprowy Wierch (2370 m asl).

*Other photographs:* Zawrat (2158 m asl, seen from the Dolina Pięciu Stawów Polskich). The traverse along the slopes of Kołowa Czuba (2105 m asl) and Mały Kozi Wierch (Little Goat's Wierch – 2228 m asl) towards Zawrat. The blue trail leads from Przedni Staw and Wielki Staw to Dolina Gąsienicowa (Gąsienice Valley).

***Dolinka Pusta (Empty Valley)*** *is a post-glacier dale above the level of Dolina Pięciu Stawów Polskich (the Valley of Five Polish Ponds). In its lower parts it is laden with large granite boulders, while in the upper parts are covered with scree.*

*Ridges from Kozi Wierch and Kołowa Czuba tower above the valley. On the South the valley is closed by a moraine, that originated near Czarny Staw Polski (the Black Polish Pond). On the North the encirclement is completed by a 140-metre wall of Zamarła Turnia.*

*The yellow trail to Kozia Przełęcz (Goat's Pass) and further to Dolina Gąsienicowa leads along Dolinka Pusta (Empty Valley).*

Kozia Przełęcz (2137 m asl) lays between vertical upcasts of Zamarła Turnia and Kozie Czuby (Goat's Crest). It is high and narrow, filled with wet mylonite – a soft rock crushed during the formation of the valley.

The yellow trail leads from Kozia Prełęcz to Zmarzły Staw (the Frozen Pond – 40 min), while the red trail leads to Kozi Wierch (over 1 h) providing you turn right, or through a long ladder to Zawrat (1 h) if you turn left.

**Zawrat**
A 2-hour-long walk from Przedni Staw (the Frontal Pond), along the blue trail through Kołowa Czuba to Zawrat.

The blue trail from the hostel by Przedni Staw leading through Dolina Pięciu Stawów (The Valley of Five Polish Ponds) is the main trail, from which other trails branch off. It runs along the shores of Przedni Staw (the Frontal Pond), Mały Staw (the Small Pond) and Wielki Staw (the Great Pond), then below the moraine of Czarny Staw (the Black Pond), to Wyżnie Solnisko and crosses the ridge of Kołowa Czuba. We are at the threshold of Dolinka pod Kołem (The Valley under the Wheel). To the West we can see Wole Oko (Ox's Eye) and, located slightly higher, Zadni Staw (the Rear Pond). Other ponds of Dolina Pięciu Stawów (The Valley of Five Polish Ponds) are also visible. Further on, the trail leads along a wide, grassy traverse below Mały Kozi Wierch (Little Goat's Wierch). Without major difficulties we reach Zawrat. We are now at 2159 m asl, between Zawratowa Turnia (Zawratowa Crag) and Mały Kozi Wierch.

From Zawrat the blue trail leads into Dolina Gąsienicowa (Gąsienice Valley). The red trail marks the beginning of Orla Perć (Eagle's Mountain Path) if you turn left, or will take you to Świnica (1 h) and Kasprowy Wierch (2 h 30 min) if you choose to turn right.

*The upper part of Dolina Pięciu Stawów Polskich (The Valley of Five Polish Ponds).*
***Zadni Staw (the Rear Pond) and Czarny Staw Polski (the Black Polish Pond)*** *lay below the ridge ranging from Świnica to Walentkowy Wierch (2156m asl). The red trail from the Slovak Dolina Cicha (Silent Valley) leads along Gladka Przełęcz (Smooth Pass - 1994m asl) visible on this picture. Above Czarny Staw lays the ridge of Kotelnica.*

# Dolina Suchej Wody (Dry Water Valley)

During the warm-up after the last glacier-period, a large glacier neighbouring Dolina Pięciu Stawów (The Valley of Five Polish Ponds) started to recede. Other glaciers in the region, the ones of Rybi Potok (the Fish' Stream) and Dolina Waksmundzka (Waksmundzka Valley), also commenced their retreat. The massifs of Opalone and Miedziane were created by the receding glaciers of these valleys. A new vast valley of Sucha Woda (Dry Water) river was created between the glaciers of Dolina Pięciu Stawów, Dolina Waksmundzka, Dolina Suchej Wody (Dry Water Valley) and Dolina Bystrej (Bystra Valley). These were the times of formation. The outlet of Dolina Suchej Wody was fenced off by a terminal moraine and numerous small ponds developed. For example **Toporowe Stawy** (the Toporowe Ponds). The lower one at 1089 m asl, 5,9 m deep, covering 0,6 ha, and the upper, much smaller and much shallower. The area of Toporowe Stawy is now a strict nature preserve, called Rezerwat Toporowe Stawy (Toporowe Ponds Nature Preserve).

Dolina Gąsienicowa (Gąsienice Valley) and Dolina Pańszczycy (Pańszczyca Valley), with the shoulder of Żółta Turnia (Yellow Crag) between them, are the extensions of Dolina Suchej Wody. They begin by the threshold which closes the latter from the South. Dolina Suchej Wody is a border-valley, a junction point of the crystalic massif of the High Tatra with the sedimentary, calcium-dolomite Western Tatra. This meeting takes place in the lower level of the valley near Liliowe pass – a contractual border between the High and the Western Tatra.

**A road to Hala Gąsienicowa** (Gąsienice Coom) leads along the bottom of Dolina Suchej Wody (Dry Water Valley). The trail starts on the road to Morskie Oko, above a forester's lodge called „Brzezina". The road to Hala Gąsienicowa originates to the South from here. It

*The view of Dolina Gąsienicowa (Gąsienica Valley) from Kasprowy Wierch: Granaty (Skrajny – 2225 m asl, Pośredni – 2234 m asl, Zadni – 2240 m asl), Kościelec (2155 m asl), Zadni Kościelec (2162 m asl – with Mylna Przełęcz (Delusive Pass)), Kozi Wierch (2291 m asl), Zawratowa Turnia (2247 m asl), Świnica (2301 m asl).*
*The path (yellow trail) on the right hand side leads form Sucha Przełęcz (Dry Pass) below Kasprowy Wierch to Hala Gąsienicowa (Gąsienice Coom).*

leads through old, spruce forests, crosses a moraine and Sucha Woda (Dry Water) – a stream which makes its way along the bottom of the valley from Zielony Staw (the Green Pond) below Liliowe (Made of Lilies). On the way you will cross a glade called **Psia Trawka** (Dog's Grass), where the path intersects with the red trail from Toporowa Cyrhla to Roztoka.

The path also leads through a mountaineers' camp located on Rąbaniska. After few minutes of walking from here you will be standing by the hostel on Hala Gąsienicowa. The time needed to reach the hostel from Brzeziny is under 2 hours.

Kuźnice (1010 m asl) is the main starting point for most tourist trails into Dolina Gąsienicowa (Gąsienice Valley) and Dolina Bystrej (Bystra Valley). Two trails lead from here to Przełęcz między Kopami (The Pass between the Piles – 1499 m asl), where they join and together run along a wide foot-path to a hostel called Murowaniec. Most trails leading through Dolina Gąsienicowa originate here.

## Nosal

A 1-hour-long walk from Kuźnice, along the green trail, through Nosalowa Przełęcz and Przewodników Tatrzańskich street.

The trail begins in Kuźnice, on the far-side of the bridge over Bystra and to the left. Initially it is accompanied by the blue trail, which branches off on Boczań. The path reaches Nosalowa Przełęcz (Nosalowa Pass – 1103 m asl). A ski trail from Hala Gąsienicowa (Gąsienice Coom) to Kuźnice runs along this pass during the Winter. The yellow trail turns right on the pass and leads through Dolina Olczyska (Olczyska Valley) to Jaszczurówka. The approximate time to complete this walk is 1 hour.

Sedimentary, calcium-dolomite rocks of Nosal summit (1206 m asl) tower above the pass, while steep gullies stretch below it. The excursion to Nosal is very relaxing and can be treated as an acclimatisation walk.

Nosal is located between Dolina Olczyska and Dolina Bystrej (Bystra Valley). A ski trail leads down the Northern slope with a chair-lift just beside it.

Within few minutes we walk down towards a dam on the river Bystra, which we cross via a bridge. There is a highlanders' snack-bar nearby.

## Dolina Jaworzynki (Jaworzynka Valley)

A 1-hour-45-minute-long walk from Kuźnice, along the yellow trail, through Polana Jaworzynki and Karczmisko.

The trail begins in Kuźnice, after crossing the bridge over Bystra, and turns to the right. We climb beside a water intake point and up the side of a moraine. After exiting the forest we reach Polana Jaworzynka (Jaworzynka Glade), a former sheep-run. Only few shacks and benches had been placed here. These elements along with the flat bottom of the valley make this trail an effortless one. Potok Jaworzynka (the Jaworzynka Stream) flows through the middle of the valley. During periods of drought some of its parts disappear.

Dolina Jaworzynki (Jaworzynka Valley), a branch of Dolina Bystrej (Bystra Valley), is surrounded from the South by Jaworzyńskie Czoła (Jaworzynka Foreheads) and jagged Jaworzyńskie Turnie (Jaworzynka Crags). From the North, the side of Boczania and Skupniów Upłaz tower above the valley, while its encirclement is completed by Kopa Magury (1704 m asl), made of calcium rocks.

Before the track enters a forest in its upper part, the valley splits into Długi Żleb (Long Gully), leading to Skupniów Upłaz, and Wielka Królowa Kopa (Great Queen Pile – 1531 m asl). Żleb pod Czerwienicą (the Gully below Czerwienica) breaks off to the South-east

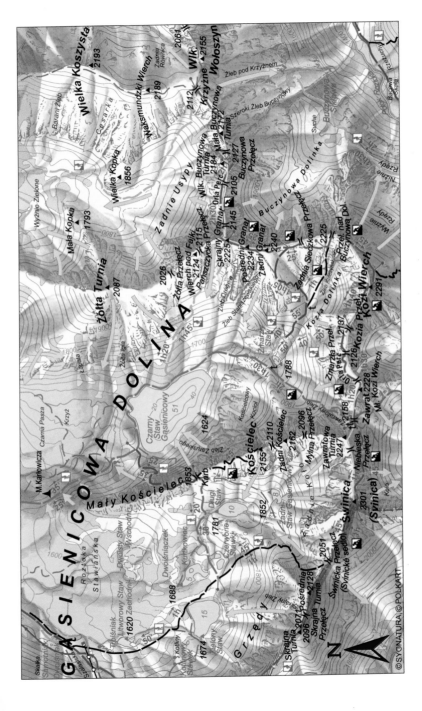

and ends high between Mała Królowa Kopa (Little Queen Pile – 1577 m asl) and Kopa Magury. Iron ore used to be mined in this gully. At first, the trail leads along a steep track through a forest-covered ridge between these gullies. Later the forest changes into dwarf-mountain-pines while the trail reaches Przełęcz pomiędzy Kopami (Pass between the Piles)

**Boczań, Skupniów Upłaz**
A 1-hour-45-minute-long walk from Kuźnice, along the blue trail, through the ridge above the valleys and Karczmisko.

The trail begins in Kuźnice, across the bridge over Bystra and leads along a wide forest road through Boczań (1224 m asl), to Skupniów Upłaz. Initially we make our way through white dolomite rocks and later through typical for this area, wet, red loam slates. We are now walking along a ridge, which divides Dolina Jaworzynki (Jaworzynka Valley) from Dolina Olczyskiej (Olczyska Valley). From the ridge you can see Dolina Bystrej (Bystra Valley) with Giewont and Podtatrze.

On the pass between Kopy (the Piles) the blue trail is joined by the yellow trail coming from Dolina Jaworzynki. We are at 1499m asl, on a slightly monarchic Królowa Równia (Queen of Planes), accompanied by Wielka Królowa Kopa (Great Queen Pile) and Mała Królowa Kopa (Little Queen Pile). The summits of the two mountains were rounded by the glacier.

**We are on a natural border between granite and calcium-dolomite sediment. In a place where High Tatra meet Western Tatra.** The mountain range from the East of Królowa Równia, through the Eastern slopes of Kopa Magura, Uhroć Kasprowy, Kasprowy Wierch with Liliowe pass is a border line. Although we are in a national park, between the East and the West, there are no custom officials. From Królowa Równia we can see the upper part of Dolina Suchej Wody with its rocky, granite branches: the smaller one to the East – Dolina Pańszczycy – and the Western one, laying on the country's border – Dolina Gąsienicowa (Gąsienice Valley).

*Dolina Jaworzynki (Jaworzynka Valley). A convenient connection between Kuźnice and Hala Gąsienicowa (Gąsienice Coom).*

**Dolina Jaworzynki (Jaworzynka Valley)** *lays between Boczań with Skupniów Upłaz (the photo below) and Jaworzyńskie Czoła (Jaworzyńskie Foreheads) with Jaworzyńskie Turnie (Jaworzynka Crags). On its ends it is closed by Królowa Kopa (Queen Pile) and Kopa Magury (1704 m asl). Polana Jaworzynki (Jaworzynka Glade) in the lower part of the* valley *is a perfect place for walks. Numerous wooden shacks make this terrain more interesting. In the past, the upper part of the valley was used for iron ore mining. Hence, today you can find some old adits there. The fragile, white rocks along the yellow trail to Dolina Gąsienicowa are dolomites. You can find such rocks all around Dolina Jaworzynki.*

The time needed for completing the walk from Przełęcz między Kopami (The Pass between the Piles) to Murowaniec is around 25 min.

## Dolina Gąsienicowa (Gąsienice Valley)

The boundaries of Dolina Gąsienicowa are clearly outlined by the ridges around it. In the East, the ridge of Żółta Turnia (Yellow Crag – 2087 m asl), which converges with Skrajny Granat (Extreme Granade – 2225 m asl), leads South to Kozi Wierch (2291 m asl). Here it turns at an almost right angle and runs through Mały Kozi Wierch (2228 m asl) to Świnica (2301 m asl) and further through Liliowe (1952 m asl) to Kasprowy Wierch (1987 m asl). The North-eastern side of the valley is depicted by the shoulder of Kasprowy Wierch with Kasprowy Uhroć (1852 m asl), which reaches the area above Kopa Magura (1704 m asl). In the North the valley's boundary leads along Las Gąsienicowy (Gąsienice Forest), below the hostel, in the spot where Czarny Potok (the Black Stream) joins Sucha Woda (Dry Water) at 1425 m asl.

The ridge of Kościelce halves Dolina Gąsienicowa. It stretches to the North from Zawratowa Turnia (Zawratowa Crag – 2247 m asl), towards Kościelec (2155 m asl) and the long ridge of Mały Kościelec (Small Kościelec), which disappears on the edge of Gąsienicowy Las (Gąsienice Forest). The two parts of Dolina Gąsienicowa, divided by the ridge of Kościelce, are: Czarna Dolina Gąsienicowa (Black Gąsienice Valley) with Czarny Staw (the Black Pond) and Zmarzły Staw (the Frozen Pond), and Zielona Dolina Gąsienicowa (Green Gąsienice Valley) along with a group of ponds of which the most significant is Zielony Staw (Green Pond). The list of other valleys attached to Dolina Gąsienicowa includes: Dolina Pańszczycy, Dolina Pięciu Stawów Polskich (The Valley of Five Polish Ponds), the great Slovak Dolina Cicha (Quiet Valley) and Dolina Kasprowa, which is a part of Western Tatra. The highest summit in the valley's vicinity is Świnica. The vast Hala Gąsienicowa (Gąsienice Coom) lays above the

*Betlejemka, a training centre of Polish Mountaineers' Association – the School of Mountaineering.*

**Giewont** seen from the upper part of the yellow trail.

**Dolina Jaworzynki** as seen from Przełęcz między Kopami (The Pass between the Piles).

**Przełęcz między Kopami (The Pass between the Piles – 1499 m asl)** is a junction point of two tourist trails form Kuźnice (1010 m asl): the yellow one, that leads through Dolina Jaworzynki (Jaworzynka Valley) and the blue one through Boczań and Skupniów Upłaz. The photograph depicts the final part of the blue trail.

upper edge of the forest. In the past, this was a sheep-run. Today, just a few buildings stand here. The most important of them is the hostel, called Murowaniec. Other structures include the building of Szkoła Taternictwa Polskiego Związku Alpinizmu w Betlejemce (The Polish Mountaineering Association's School of Mountaineering in Betlejemka), which we pass when walking down from Królowa Równia, a forester's lodge and a meteorological station.

**Murowaniec** – a tourist hostel located in the heart of Hala Gąsienicowa at 1500 m asl. It is large building, which can accommodate 109 guests in rooms for 3, 4, or 5 people. The hostel is crowded mainly in Summer and Winter seasons. All tourist trails, which exist around the valley, are depicted on a sign-post in front of the building.

### Czarny Staw Gąsienicowy (the Black Gąsienice Pond)

A 35-minute-long walk from Murowaniec, along the blue trail, through Kamień Karłowicza and the eastern slopes of Kościelec.

After reaching Czarny Staw Gąsienicowy the blue trail leads to Zawrat – a pass, which is a point of origin of three tracks. The first heads East and leads to Orla Perć, through a ridge over Dolina Gąsienicowa (Gąsienice Valley) and Dolina Pańszczycy (Pańszczyca Valley). The second leads due South to Dolina Pięciu Stawów Polskich (The Valley of Five Polish Ponds) and further to Dolina Roztoki (Roztoka Valley) or Dolina Rybiego Potoku (the Fish's Stream Valley). The last one heading West, runs through Świnica and Liliowe (Made of Lilies) to the Western Tatra.

The trail begins at the doorstep of the hostel. The track leads Southwards along a rocky path, among tall dwarf-mountain-pines. We are walking along a smooth and grassy slope of Mały Kościelec (Small Kościelec) ridge. Below the trail, on the left hand side we can see **Kamień Karłowicza** (Karłowicz's Stone), placed here in memory of the great Polish composer,

*„Murowaniec" tourist hostel on Hala Gąsienicowa (Gąsienice Coom). The junction of all trails, which lead through Dolina Gąsienicowa (Gąsienice Valley).*

The path from Murowaniec on Hala Gąsienicowa to Czarny Staw Gąsienicowy (the Black Gąsienice Pond) traverses the side of Mały Kościelec (Little Kościelec). Mieczysław Karłowicz, the great Polish composer, was killed here by a snow avalanche, that came down the Eastern slope of Mały Kościelec. A memorial stone with an inscription was placed just below the path in memory of this tragedy. The engraving says: „Nie wszystek umrę" (I shall not die entirely).

The upper photo: above Czarny Staw (the Black Pond).

The bottom photo: traversing the slopes of Mały Kościelec towards Czarny Staw.

who was killed in this spot by an avalanche in February 1909. As we approach a rock threshold, the waters of Czarny Staw (the Black Pond) behind it become visible. On the right, we can see rifts in the granite wall of Kościelec, which towers above the pond with a 530-metre-high cliff.

**Czarny Staw** lays at 1620 m asl. It is surrounded by Żółta Turnia (Yellow Crag), Wierch pod Fajki (2135 m asl) and Skrajny Granat (Extreme Granate). From the South it is closed by the steep walls of Kościelcowy Kocioł (Kościelec Dale), overlooked by the pyramid of Kościelec.

Czarny Staw is one of the largest ponds in Dolina Gąsienicowa (Gąsienice Valley) and with its area of 17,79 ha holds the fifth place in the ranking of the largest ponds in Tatra. It is 51 metres deep, a fact worth remembering when standing on the shore. The merky waters of Czarny Staw, or the 25 metres deeper Morskie Oko, owe its colour to an algae called Cyanophyceae. Other life forms inhabiting this pond include trout. This fish, however, was introduced to this habitat artificially. A stream flows through the threshold on the North. This is Czarny Potok (the Black Stream), which flows down to Sucha Woda (Dry Water) river. It is partially visible from the slope of Mały Kościelec. Not far away from the Northern shore of the pond, on the opposite side to the outlet of Czarny Potok, you can find a small rocky island, which rises around a metre above the water-level and is covered with dwarf-mountain-pines.

### Karb

A 30-minute-long walk from Czarny Staw along the green trail, through the pass.

The green trail to Karb breaks off from the blue trail, which leads from Murowaniec to Czarny Staw, near the rock threshold before the pond. It leads among dwarf-mountain-pines through a zigzag track on the steep Eastern slope of Mały Kościelec. Karb (1853 m asl) is a wide pass, that separates the rounded ridge of Mały Kościelec (1863 m asl) from the tall, rocky pyramid of Kościelec (2155 m asl).

*Czarny Staw Gąsienicowy (Black Gąsienice Pond – 1624 m asl).*
*The blue trail to Zawrat (2158 m asl) leads along the path around the pond, visible on the right side of the picture. On the same side you can see the separation of the yellow trail to Skrajny Granat (Extreme Granade – 2225 m asl).*

**Czarny Staw Gąsienicowy (Black Gąsienica Pond – 1624 m asl).**

The view from the pond: bottom picture (from the left hand side) – Granaty (2224 – 2240 m asl), Czarne Ściany (Black Walls), Kozi Wierch (Goat's Wierch – 2291 m asl), Kozie Czuby (2266 m asl), Kozia Przełęcz (Goat's Pass – 2137m asl) and the wall of Kościelec.

Below Kozi Wierch lays Kozia Dolina (Goat's Valley – visible on this photograph). The yellow trail to Kozia Przełęcz leads along it.

Upper photos: the view of Czarny Staw from the path to Zawrat (on the left) and from Karb (on the right).

**Zawrat**

A 2-hour-long walk from Czarny Staw, along the blue trail, through Zmarzły Staw (the Frozen Pond) and Zawratowy Żleb (The Gully of Zawrat)

The track leads initially along the Northern shore of Czarny Staw. After crossing Czarny Potok it turns into a wide path among dwarf-mountain-pines. We are walking below the Western, scree-covered slopes of Żółta Turnia (Yellow Ridge) with Kościelec towering on the right.

A yellow trail to Skrajny Granat (Extreme Granate – 1 h 45 min) branches off to the left from our path. The mountain marks the edge of Orla Perć.

The blue trail leads upwards, above the lake, towards the scree-covered gullies of Staniszewski and Drege, that fall from Granaty. The path takes us to taluses. After crossing a stream flowing from Czarny Staw (covered with a thick layer of frozen snow till late Spring), we reach a rocky dike. Zmarzły Staw (the Frozen Pond) is just behind it. We are at the foot of a 150 metre threshold created by post-glacier dales of Kościelcowy Kocioł (Kościelec Dale) and Kocioł Zmarzłego Stawu (The Dale of the Frozen Pond). The path climbs steeply and leads to the shore of Zmarzły Staw. On our way we pass a large patch of snow, which stays here usually throughout the Summer.

**Zmarzły Staw Gąsienicowy** (the Gąsienice Frozen Pond) lays at 1788 m asl in a sharply craved post-glacier dale, which hangs over the niche of Czarny Staw (the Black Pond). It is encircled by the granite walls of Kościelec, Kozie Wierchy (Goat's Wierchy) and Granaty (Granades). The pond covers 0,28 ha and is 3,7 m deep. The chilly climate of the dale in combination with high altitude and small dimensions of the pond cause Zmarzły Staw to be frozen throughout the most of the year. This is a charming place, regardless the unpleasant

*The dale of Czarny Staw Gąsienicowy.*

climatic conditions. It lays 100 metres below Zadni Staw (the Rear Pond), located on the other side of the ridge – in Dolina Pięciu Stawów Polskich. A small stream flows from Zmarzły Staw.

The yellow trail to Kozia Przełęcz branches off to the left below Zmarzły Staw (Frozen Pond), along with a green and a black one. The former leads to Zadni Granat, while the latter, to Orla Perć (Eagle's Mountain Path). The time needed to reach any of these places from Zmarzły Staw is roughly an hour.

Going down from Zmarzły Staw, the trail leads through zigzags and rocks towards the walls of Zadni Kościelec, and further to the taluses of the long **Zawratowy Żleb** (Zawrat Gully). A road to Zawrat, called Stary Zawrat (Old Zawrat), lead through here in the past. On the left, in the rocks of Mały Kozi Wierch (Little Goat's Wierch) a tourist trail was created and secured with chains and buckles. It is called Nowy Zawrat (New Zawrat). Climbing this trail takes 30 minutes, then we reach a pass. The Winter-trail leads along Stary Zawrat. A sculpture that stands on a rock shelf in the last part of Zawratowy Żleb represents Virgin Mary. It was placed here in the beginning of the XXth century. A short brake here is worth making, before the vast spaces of the pass open in front of us. Below, you can see a yellow rescue box. After the last effort of climbing the rock, we reach the level of 2159 m asl. We are now on Zawrat.

**Zawrat** (2159 m asl) – a pass between Zawratowa Turnia (The Crag of Zawrat – 2247 m asl) on the West and Mały Kozi Wierch (Little Goat's Wierch – 2228 m asl) on the East. The blue trail leads from here to Dolina Pięciu Stawów Polskich (The Valley of Five Polish Ponds) and further to Morskie Oko or Dolina Roztoki (Roztoka Valley). The path to Dolina Pięciu Stawów runs along a wide traverse and crosses the upper level of Dolinka pod Kołem (The Valley under the Wheel). In terms of difficulty it differs a lot from the path to Zawrat along Zawratowy Żleb.

*Dusk in Dolina Gąsienicowa.*

*Upper photo: the dale of the Frozen Pond. The trails to Kozia Przełęcz (Goat's Pass – yellow) and Zadni Granat (Rear Granade – green) lead above it.*

*The view of Kościelec and Granaty from the path leading from Kasprowy Wierch to Murowaniec (the photo on the right).*

*Bottom picture: Zmarzły Staw (the Frozen Pond) seen from the path to Zawrat and the peaks of Żółta Turnia (Yellow Crag), Wierch pod Fajki and Granaty. To the right from Zmarzły Staw lays the threshold of Kozia Dolina (Goat's Valley).*

113

The pass marks the beginning of Orla Perć, which stretches to the East, while to the West it leads to Świnica.

**Kozia Przełęcz**
A 1-hour-30minute-long walk from Czarny Staw, along the blue trail, through Zmarzły Staw and Kozia Dolinka.

Initially the path from Czarny Staw to Kozia Przełęcz is the blue trail to Zawrat. Before Zmarzly Staw, below the rock threshold, we turn onto a yellow trail, which breaks to the left. The path climbs above Kocioł Zmarzłego Stawu and leads onto a threshold of Kozia Dolinka.

The valley lays between the walls of Kozie Wierchy and Granaty. It is filled with scree and various, partially smoothened rocks. Although this is not a mountain climb, the trail leads through open terrain.

In its last sections the yellow trail climbs up to the rocky shelves of Zamarła Turnia. Then it leads to the gully falling from Kozia Przełęcz. After climbing up the gully we reach **Kozia Przełęcz** at 2137 m asl. It lays between Zamarła Turnia and Kozie Czuby. From here the yellow trail goes down into Dolina Pięciu Stawów Polskich and Wyżnie Solnisko where it reunites with the blue trail from Zawrat. This path is by all means worth recommending.

**Skrajny Granat (Extreme Granade)**
A 2-hour-long walk along the yellow trail.

The scree-covered yellow trail to Skrajny Granat branches off from the blue trail to Zawrat in the middle of the Eastern shore of Czarny Staw Gąsienicowy (the Black

*Żółta Turnia (Yellow Crag – 2087 m asl).*
*Zawrat (the bottom picture), a view of Żółta Turnia and the sides of Granaty*
*The path to Zawrat from Kotlina Zmarzłego Stawu (the Frozen Pond's Dale); the scree covered gully below the pass is called Stary Zawrat (Old Zawrat – the photo on the right).*

114

Gąsienice Pond). A path in the lower part leads through dwarf-mountain-pines along the Western slope of Żółta Turnia (Yellow Crag – 2087 m asl). We move on, cross a gully from Żółta Przełęcz and walk onto a rocky slope of Wierch pod Fajki (2135 m asl). It consists of a number of jagged crags which lay between Skrajny Granat and Żółta Turnia. After crossing another scree-covered gully falling from Pańszczycka Przełęcz (2115 m asl) we walk into a wall of Skrajny Granat. After forcing it, we reach the summit – 2225 m asl.

**Skrajny Granat** is a junction-summit – it towers above three valleys: Dolina Gąsienicowa (Gąsienice Valley), Dolina Pańszczycy (Pańszczyca Valley) and Dolina Buczynowa (Beech Valley). It is also a meeting place of three ridges: from the South – the ridge stretching from the remaining Granades and Kozie Wierchy (Goat's Wierchy), from the North – the ridge from Wierch pod Fajki and Żółta Turnia, and finally from the East – the ridge from Wielka Buczynowa Turnia (Great Beech Crag) and Krzyżne.

### Zadni Granat (Rear Granade)
A 2-hour-long walk from Czarny Staw, along the blue, yellow and green trails.

From Czarny Staw we walk along the blue trail, which leads to Zawrat, all the way to Zmarzły Staw. Here, the yellow trail branches off to the left and we turn with it. The path climbs through Kozia Dolina to a junction of trails. The yellow trail leads to Kozia Przełęcz, while a new trail, the green one, will take us through scree-covered sides and walls of Zadni Granat (2240 m asl) to finally meet Orla Perć. From here we walk along the red trail, up the ridge, towards the peak. This track can be treated as a relatively easy connection to and from Orla Perć.

*Orla Perć (Eagle's Mountain Path) – the red trail*
  *The section from Zawrat to Zamarła Turnia. Świnica towers in the background, Zadni Kościelec (Rear Kościelec) and Przełęcz Mylna (Delusive Pass) on the right (upper photo).*
  *Climbing up Orla Perć in the wall of Zamarła Turnia onto Kozia Przełęcz (Goat's Pass) (photos on the right and below).*

**Żleb Kulczyńskiego (Kulczyński's Gully)**
An over 2-hour-long walk from Czarny
Staw, along the black trail to the ridge of
Orla Perć.

The black trail is an offshoot of the
green trail to Zadni Granat. It appears in
Kozia Dolinka and leads initially along a
path. With altitude the track gradually
changes its form into a pebbly path, which
secured with a rocky gutter leads towards a
scree-covered cone of Żleb Kulczyńskiego.
From here we climb to the junction point
with Orla Perć. A path to the right rumbles
above Buczynowa Dolinka and leads
towards Kozi Wierch and Zawrat. The red
trail turns left and leads, through a rock
chimney, onto the ridge of Zadni Granat
and Skrajny Granat.

*Alone in the granite rock.*

*Taking a rest before Kozia Przełęcz Wyżnia
(Upper Goat's Pass – 2240 m asl).*

*This climb will end on Kozi Wierch (2291
m asl).*

**Kozia Przełęcz (Goat's Pass – 2137 m asl –** the photo on the upper right) a thin pass connecting Kozia Dolina (Goat's Valley) with Dolinka Pusta (Empty Valley). It lays between Zamarła Turnia (2179 m asl) and Kozie Szczyty (Goat's Summits – 2266 m asl).

The photo on the left: a secured trail to Kozia Przełęcz (Goat's Pass) along the wall of Zamarła Turnia.

The picture on the bottom: the yellow trail to the Dolina Pięciu Stawów Polskich (The Valley of Five Polish Ponds). The scree covered terrain of Dolinka Pusta in the background.

The rocky peak of the highest summit, that lays totally on the Polish side – **Kozi Wierch (2291 m asl)**.

The photo beside: the red trail below the peak.

The bottom picture: Dolina Gąsienicowa (Gąsienice Valley) in mist on the right. On the left you can see Zadni Staw (the Rear Pond) in Dolina Pięciu Stawów Polskich (The Valley of Five Polish Ponds) and the Slovak Walentkowy Wierch (2156 m asl), the wall of which falls into the valley.

Orla Perć (Eagle's Mountain Path) and the red ridge-trail in the foreground.

# Orla Perć
## (Eagle's Mountain Path)

Zawrat, Mały Kozi Wierch (Little Goat's Pinnacle), Zamarła Turnia, Kozia Przełęcz (Goats' Pass), Kozie Czuby (Goats' Peaks), Kozi Wierch (Goat's Wierch), Buczynowa Strażnica (Buczynowa Watch-tower), Czarne Ściany (Black Walls), Zadni Granat (Rear Granade), Pośredni Granat (Middle Granade), Skrajny Granat (Extreme Granade), Granacka Przełęcz (Granade Pass), Orla Baszta (Eagle's Tower), Przełęcz Nowickiego (Nowicki's Pass), Wielka Buczynowa Turnia (Great Beech Crag), Mała Buczynowa Turnia (Small Beech Crag), Krzyżne.

The time needed to walk from Zawrat to Krzyżne, along the red trail, is approximately 6 hours. But you need additional 6 hours for the way to and from the ridge, providing that you are walking from Zakopane or Bukowina. All in all, you should reserve at least 12 hours for the whole excursion. Bearing in mind the fact

*The mountain path leading along the walls of Zadni Granat (Rear Granade). After traversing the granite walls of Granaty we will be able to see the dale of Czarny Staw Gąsienicowy (the Black Gąsienica Pond).*

*Orla Perć (Eagle's Mountain Path) above Żleb Kulczyńskiego (Kulczyński's Gully) leads through a rock-chimney into Czarne Ściany (Black Walls). You can walk through Żleb Kulczyńskiego along the black trail, then take the green trail to Zmarzły Staw (the Frozen Pond) and further to Czarny Staw (the Black Pond).*

121

that Summer-days are long and providing that our condition is sufficient for such an exercise, we can freely venture out.

After making a short break on Zawrat, we move on to conquer Orla Perć. If we came from Hala Gąsienicowa, we turn left. From Dolina Pięciu Stawów, we turn right and finally, if we have just been on Świnica, then we simply keep walking along the red trail.

After 15 minutes Mały Kozi Wierch (Little Goat's Wierch – 2228 m asl) appears before us. We make the way up through a rocky ridge. On our way we pass a couple of rather low, but wide peaks. Mały Kozi Wierch is the third of them. The ridge of Kołowa Czuba (2105 m asl) meets Orla Perć (Eagle's Mountain Path) from the South. It separates the upper level of Dolina Pięciu Stawów (The Valley of Five Polish Ponds) into two smaller valleys: Dolina pod Kołem (The Valley under the Wheel) and Dolina Pusta (Empty Valley). The ridge, that we are on now, rises above these valleys with 400-metre-high walls. From Mały Kozi Wierch

*Skrajny Granat (Extreme Granade – 2225 m asl) – a junction point if three ridges: one ranging from Granaty, another from Żółta Turnia (Yellow Crag – 2087 m asl) and the last one from the Eastern part of Orla Perć (Eagle's Mountain Path) and heading towards Wielka Buczynowa Turnia (Great Beech Crag – 2184 m asl).*

*The meeting of Orla Perć and the green trail from Zmarzły Staw (the Frozen Pond) before Zadni Granat (Rear Granade).*

***The Eastern part of Orla Perć (Eagle's Mountain Path)***

Upper picture: the Eastern part of Orla Perć with the mist crawling from Dolina Gąsienicowa.

The picture on the bottom depicts **Dolinka Buczynowa (Beech Valley)**. Laying at 1700-1950 m asl, it constitutes the upper part of Dolina Roztoki (Roztoka Valley). A red tourist trail leads above the valley. The yellow trail connecting Krzyżne and Dolina Pięciu Stawów Polskich (the Valley of Five Polish Ponds) leads through the bottom of the valley. In the background you can see a rock threshold – Stawiarska Ściana (Stawiarska Wall) – along with Przedni Staw (the Frontal Pond).

we walk towards the Southern side of the ridge, to a small pass and further to a steep, craved gully. The trail rambles through the gully and leads to the Northern side above Kozia Dolinka. This section is well secured with chains, especially when the snow still lays on the track. If there is too much snow for us to handle, we should turn back. Risk is not worth taking here.

We are on the Northern rocky shelves of Zmarzłe Czuby. On the South, these two crags end with steep walls, quite popular among mountain-climbers. We reach the top of the crag. From here, aided by buckles and chains, we make our way down a steep wall, then along a precipice just below the crag to finally reach Zmarzła Przełęcz (Frozen Pass) at 2126 m asl. The pass greets us with a granite club – a tall jag. A short break here is recommended. In the meantime we may take a look at the Southern wall of Zamarła Turnia. We leave Zmarzła Przełęcz through two large, rock terraces of the Northern wall of Zamarła Turnia (2179 m asl), which rise above Zmarzły Staw (the Frozen Pond). After struggling through the first scree-covered terrace we climb, using the aids provided, to the second. From here we need to climb to the upper part of this terrace. Here we can stop over a precipice, a smooth, vertical wall, that leads down to **Kozia Przełęcz**.

We are almost in the middle of the Western part of Orla Perć, between Zawrat and Kozi Wierch. To the South lays Dolinka Pusta, while to the North, Kozia Dolinka. The two valleys are linked by the yellow trail, which leads through Kozia Przełęcz (Goats' Pass).

It takes 1 hour and 20 minutes to walk from Zawrat to Kozia Przełęcz.

The next part of Orla Perć awaits us. From Kozia Przełęcz we head for Kozi Wierch. This part of our trip should take around 1 h 30 min. Some climbing will be necessary.

After crossing a narrow and deep Kozia Przełęcz, the trail leads to the South side, towards the walls of Kozie Czuby. Using chains and other aids we climb up a gully. The trail heads for the Northern side and leads to Czuby, with their summit at 2266 m asl. From the peak of Kozie Czuby we climb down along a steep crevasse to Kozia Przełęcz Wyżnia (2240 m asl). Our next climb to Kozi Wierch can be seen very well from here. It leads through a

*The Eastern part of Orla Perć (Eagle's Mountain Path) that traverses above Buczynowa Dolinka (Beech Valley) ending with **Krzyżne** pass (**2122 m asl**, the photo on the right).*

The Eastern part of Orla Perć leads on one side above Dolina Roztoki, while on the other rises above **Dolina Pańszczyca** – an extension of Dolina Suchej Wody Gąsienicowej (The Valley of Dry Gąsienice Water).

The yellow trail leads down into Krzyżne valley. The trail, in its upper parts, leads among great boulders to Czerwony Staw (the Red Pond – 1654m asl) and further, among dwarf-mountain-pines and forests, to Murowaniec.

The green trail to Polana Waksmundzka (Waksmundzka Glade – 1365-1400 m asl) leads through the bottom of the valley.

ridge along a long and steep gully, which ends at the summit rocks. We are on the highest peak, which lays entirely on the Polish side – **Kozi Wierch** – 2291 m asl. It constitutes the culmination of Orla Perć (Eagle's Mountain Path). Behold, the beautiful view of High Tatra in all its splendour. The time required to walk from Zawrat to Kozi Wierch is over 2 h 30 min.

The next section of Orla Perć, the middle one, is between Kozi Wierch and Skrajny Granat. The distance takes a little under 2 hours to walk. The most demanding climbing-paths lay behind us. The track will now lead along the ridge, above Dolinka Buczynowa and Kozia Dolinka.

The red trail from Kozi Wierch runs down the rocky path towards the Southern slope and Dolina Pięciu Stawów. The black trail leading to Wielki Staw Polski branches off here. The mountain-pass leads further to Przełęczka nad Doliną Buczynową (Little Pass above Beech Valley – 2225 m asl). From here we walk to the Northern side of the rib. We are below the ridge of Czarne Ściany (Black Walls – 2245 m asl) and head for the precipices of **Żleb Kulczyńskiego**. It is a wide gully, carved in its lower parts, which falls towards Zmarzły Staw. The pond can be reached via the black trail.

We struggle through Żleb Kulczyńskiego along its upper parts. Then we make our way down to a rock threshold, turn right, climb up a steep rock chimney and head for Zadnia Sieczkowa Przełączka (Rear Sieczkowa Pass – 2190 m asl). This pass fences off Czarne Ściany (Black Walls) from Zadni Granat (Rear Granade).

We walk up the Western slope of Zadni Granat. The green trail to Zmarzły Staw diverges to the left. After few minutes we reach **Zadni Granat** (2240 m asl). There is a cross on the summit. As we traverse the slopes of Granades we should bear in our minds the fact that they are often carved by precipices. Hence making any shortcuts is not recommended.

From Zadni Granat we head for the Eastern slopes. Then after reaching Pośrednia Sieczkowa Przełączka (Middle Sieczkowa Pass – 2218 m asl) we walk directly across the ridge to Pośredni Granat (2234 m asl). From the peak we walk along a narrow rib, over a crevasse and onto Skrajna Sieczkowa Przełączka (Extreme Sieczkowa Pass – 2200 m asl). We move on through a steep scree-covered path and reach the Northern peak of Granades – **Skrajny Granat** (2225 m asl). A yellow trail leads from the summit to Czarny Staw.

We enter the last, Eastern part of Orla Perć. We reach a downcast of the ridge and through an open steep slope we go down to Granacka Przełęcz (Granade Pass – 2145 m asl). At this point the ridge runs along the Northern side of Orla Perć (Eagle's Mountain Path), above Dolina Pańszczycy. We traverse the steep Northern walls of Orle Turniczki (secured path) and reach a small pass covered with rocks and grass, just under the summit of Orla Baszta (Eagle's Tower – 2177 m asl). We move on to the South side. Below us lays Dolinka Buczynowa (Beech Valley), we can see Stawiarska Ściana (Stawiarska Wall) and Przedni Staw (the Frontal Pond) above it. The trail descends. It reaches a steep, secured, 12-metre-high chimney, which ends with a small pass, called Pościel Jasińskiego (Jasiński's Bedding). The pass is located above a precipice, which is said to claim the life of a poacher, who got lost in these areas.

Further on we walk along the ridge connecting Orla Baszta (Eagle's Tower) with Wielka Buczynowa Turnia (Great Beech Crag). The path runs through open terrain. In its middle lays Przełęcz Nowickiego (2105 m asl), which owes its name to the poet Franciszek H. Nowicki. He was the initiator and the biggest supporter of the plan of creating a trail to Orla Perć. A goal, which is no longer attainable.

The trail doesn't lead along the edge of Wielka Buczynowa Turnia (2184 m asl), but through its Southern side. It descends towards the great scree-covered gully, that falls from Buczynowa Przełęcz (Beech Pass – 2127 m asl). We cross the gully in its lower part and then traverse up a steep slope onto Mała Buczynowa Turnia (Small Beech Crag – 2172 m asl). The path leads further down the main ridge, through its Southern side, to **Krzyżne** (2112 m asl). On the right we can see the yellow trail track to Dolina Pięciu Stawów Polskich (The Valley of Five

***Kościelec (2155 m asl).*** *A pyramid-shaped massif that divides Dolina Gąsienicowa into: the Eastern part – Czarna Dolina Gąsienicowa (Black Gąsienice Valley), and the Western part – Zielona Dolina Gąsienicowa (Green Gąsienice Valley) (the photo on the upper right). The massif comprises of the rib of Mały Kościelec (1863m asl) fenced off from the main summit* *by Karb (1853 m asl, the photo on the upper left). Mylna Przełęcz (Delusive Pass) laying between Kościelec (2162 m asl) and Zawratowa Turnia (Zawratowa Crag – 2247 m asl) continues the separation. The bottom picture depicts the rib from Mały Kościelec to Przełęcz Mylna. Długi Staw Gąsienicowy (Long Gąsienice Pond) is visible below Karb.*

Polish Ponds), leading through the wide Żleb pod Krzyżnem (The Gully under Krzyżne). Krzyżne ends the trail of Orla Perć (Eagle's Mountain Path). Six hours are needed to walk from Zawrat to the pass. The yellow trail, which turns left on Krzyżne, leads to Hala Gąsienicowa (Gąsienice Coom) through Dolina Pańszczycy and takes approximately 2 h 30 min.

## Dolina Pańszczycy (Pańszczyca Valley)

A 2-hour-30-minute-long walk from Murowaniec, along the yellow trail, through Czerwony Staw (the Red Pond) and Krzyżne.

**Dolina Pańszczycy**, like Dolina Gąsienicowa (Gąsienice Valley), is a branch and the upper, Southern level of Dolina Suchej Wody (Dry Water Valley). Żółta Turnia (Yellow Crag) and Granaty (Granades) lay to the West from the valley. To the East, the massif of Koszysta, and to the South, the ridges of Buczynowe Turnie (Beech Crags). In its lower parts the valley is covered with forests and dwarf-mountain-pines, while at higher altitudes there is only grass and rocks of various shapes and sizes. Czerwony Staw (the Red Pond) lays in the middle of the valley, at 1654 m asl. On average it covers an area of 0,3 ha and is roughly one metre deep. If the water level increases the pond can change into two ponds. Pańszczycki Potok (the Pańszczycki Stream) originates in Czerwony Staw and flows through the valley, mainly under the surface.

The yellow trail, along with the green one to Polana Waksmundzka, begin on the supply road to Brzeziny, below Murowaniec.

The trail leads along a tall, spruce forest, climbing gently onto the slopes of Żółta Turnia (Yellow Crag) and into a small valley called Dubrawiska. Żółty Potok (the Yellow Stream) flows down its middle, which originates 1700 metres higher – in Żółta Turnia (Yellow Crag). The path runs along a small waterfall created by the stream. After reaching the ridge of Zadni Upłaz (Rear Terrace) we head South for Czerwony Staw (the Red Pond). The upper boundary

*Karb (1853 m asl) with the ridge of Mały Kościelec (Little Kościelec).*
*Below lay Długi Staw (the Long Pond) and Kurtkowiec. The green trail from Zielony Staw (the Green Pond) leads between them onto a pass, from which it heads for Czarny Staw Gąsienicowy (the Black Gąsienice Pond).*

of dwarf-mountain-pines lays below. The track leads deeper into the quiet valley through immense amounts of rocks and stones. Great fields of snow form here during the Winter. The trail leads along the arm of Wielka Koszysta (2193 m asl). It omits the peak of Wielka Kopka (1856 m asl) and zigzags through a scree-covered terrain to finally reach Krzyżne.

## Dolina Stawów Gąsienicowych (The Valley of Gąsienice Ponds)

The Western part of Dolina Gąsienicowa, to the South of Murowaniec, is littered with numerous ponds, of various shapes and sizes, laying at different altitudes. Some of them are partially concealed behind tall dwarf-pines. This is Dolina Stawów Gąsienicowych, also know as Zielona Dolina Gąsienicowa (Green Gąsienice Valley).

It is surrounded by the ribs of Kościelce and the ridge from Świnica to Kasprowy Wierch and Uhrocie Kasprowe. The border between the crystalic High Tatra and sedimentary Western Tatra mountains runs right through the middle of Dolina Stawów Gąsienicowych, to the North of Przełęcz Liliowe (The Pass of Lilies).

There are over 15 ponds in the glen of the valley. The largest and the most significant are listed below:

Zielony Staw (the Green Pond – 1672 m asl), at the feet of Skrajna Turnia (2096 m asl), covers 3,84 ha and is 15,1 m deep. Długi Staw (the Long Pond – 1783 m asl), at the feet of Kościelec, covers 1,58 ha and is 10,6 m deep. Kurtkowiec lays in the middle of the glen at 1686 m asl, covers 1,56 ha and is 4,8 m deep. Dwoisty Staw (the Dual Pond) at the feet of Mały Kościelec (Little Kościelec) comprises of two ponds which cover 1,41 ha and 0,9 ha and are respectively 9,2 m and 7,9 m deep. Zadni Staw (the Rear Pond – 1852 m asl), at the feet of Kościelec, lays at the greatest altitude of all the ponds in the glen. Its area is 0,53 ha, while it is 8 m deep. Other ponds, which bear names are: Litworowy, Troiśniak (three tiny ponds), Kotlinowy and two Czerwone Stawki (the Red Ponds).

*A view of Dolina Pięciu Stawów Polskich (The Valley of Five Polish Ponds), Miedziane (Copper – 2233 m asl) and Szpiglasowy Wierch (2172 m asl) from Świnica. In the background you can see Gierlach (2654 m asl), Rysy (2499 m asl), Wysoka (Tall – 2560 m asl), Mięguszowiecki Szczyt (Mięguszowiecki Summit – 2438 m asl) and Cubryna (2376 m asl).*

*The red trail from **Zawrat to Świnica**. It leads above Zadni Staw (the Rear Pond) in Dolina* | *Pięciu Stawów Polskich. The path is secured with numerous chains, buckles and ladders.*

*The upper parts of Świnica.*

The black trail leads through Dolina Stawów Gąsienicowych (Gąsienice Ponds Valley), from Murowaniec to Świnicka Przełęcz (Świnicka Pass – 2051 m asl). The distance takes 1 h 30 min to walk. The blue trail leads through the valley to Karb. It separates from the black trail somewhere between Kurtkowiec and Czerwone Stawki (the Red Ponds). 30 minutes are needed to reach the pass.

### Kościelec

A 45-minute-long walk from Karb, along the black trail.

The black trail from Karb, a pass between the rib of Mały Kościelec and Kościelec itself, leads through steep granite slabs, along the left edge. In the upper parts the track zigzags around rock shelves and gutters. Finally it reaches a rocky pyramid. From the summit you can clearly see the division of Dolina Gąsienicowa into two parts. Zadni Kościelec (Rear Kościelec – 2162 m asl) lays at the protraction of the ridge to the South. It is cut off from Zawratowa Turnia (Zawratowa Crag – 2247 m asl) by Przełęcz Mylna (Delusive Pass – 2096 m asl). Unfortunately the trail ends on the main summit of Kościelec, rendering the ridge between Zawrat and Świnica unattainable.

### Świnica

A 1-hour-30-minute-long walk from Zawrat to Świnica along the red trail. Then a 1-hour-long walk from Świnica to Kasprowy Wierch, also along the red trail.

The red trail heading West from Zawrat is simply an extension of Orla Perć. It leads above three great valleys: Dolina Pięciu Stawów Polskich (The Valley of Five Polish Ponds), Dolina Gąsienicowa (Gąsienice Valley) and the Slovak Dolina Cicha (Silent Valley).

*Kasprowy Wierch (1987m asl). Giewont (1894 m asl) is in the background.*

The pictures depict the main, South-eastern peak of Świnica *(2301 m asl)*. The other, North-western peak is at 2291 m asl. The main peak of Świnica is a junction point of three ridges. To the South, the ridge to Walentkowy Wierch (2156 m asl) above the Slovak Dolina Walentkowa. To the East stretches the ridge to Kozie Wierchy above Dolina Pięciu Stawów Polskich (The Valley of Five Polish Ponds), while to the West, the ridge to Pośrednia Turnia (Middle Crag – 2128 m asl) and Liliowe pass (1952 m asl) above Dolina Gąsienicowa. Below the peak stands a GOPR plate warning about the potential hazard connected with staying on the summit during a storm.

After reaching Zawrat we walk down along the red trail, then traverse the steep slope of Zawratowa Turnia (2247 m asl), falling into Dolinka pod Kołem. Throughout the most of this leg of our excursion we will be able to see Zadni Staw Polski (the Rear Polish Pond – 1890 m asl) below us. The traverse ends in a scree-covered gully, that falls from Niebieska Turnia (Blue Crag – 2262 m asl). We start to climb the Eastern ridge of Świnica, along the walls of Gąsienicowa Turnia (Gąsienice Crag – 2280 m asl). On the Southern side of Gąsienicowa Turnia, above the track, you can find a cave called Świnicka Koleba (2250 m asl). It can serve as a shelter in case of an unexpected weather-breakdown.

A series of rocky ribs and shelves, gutters and short vertical gullies in open terrain lay before us. We make our way with the aid of chains and buckles. Zadni Staw Polski (1890 m asl) lays beneath, in Dolina pod Kołem (The Valley below The Wheel). The climbout leads along the Southern sides so the rocks are pleasantly warm thanks to the sun. It is a nice farewell to the High Tatra. After reaching the last part of the steep slope we can see a GOPR (Górskie Ochotnicze Pogotowie Ratunkowe – Volunteer Mountain Rescue Service) warning plate on the wall. Few moments later we are on Świnica (2301 m asl) – the main rib of the Tatra mountains.

**Świnica** is a double-peak summit (2301, 2291 m asl) in the main ridge of Tatra. It is a junction point of three ridges. The first runs to the South, towards Walentkowy Wierch . The second, due East, to Kozi Wierch, while the third heads West for Kasprowy Wierch. The summit lays in the centre of Polish and Slovak Tatra. The red trail leads through the Southern, higher (2301 m asl) peak. The lower peak is on the North. Świnica towers above Dolina Gąsienicowa and provides tourists with some splendid sights. The summit itself is visible even from Zakopane.

After a longer stay at Świnica we move on. The North-western ridge of Świnica lays ahead. The ridge leads through Świnicka Przełęcz (Świnicka Pass) to Skrajna Przełęcz (Extreme Pass) and further through Liliowe to Kasprowy Wierch. This trail can be

*A view from **Kasprowy Wierch** (1987 m asl) at Beskid (2012 m asl), Liliowe (1952 m asl – a pass fencing the Western Tatra from the High Tatra mountains) and Świnica (2301 m asl – the first tall summit in the main ridge of the High Tatra). The photo on the right depicts Świnicka Przełęcz (Świnicka Pass – 2051 m asl). The black trail leads from here down to Dolina Gąsienicowa.*

completed in 1 h 30 min. The difference of levels at the relatively short distance between Świnica and the pass is 250 m. The track, in its upper parts, leads through open terrain.

The red trail is a link between Świnica and the main trail from Zawrat. The track leads along the Southern walls of this Granite massif, above the Slovak Dolina Walentkowa (Walentkowa Valley). After walking in open, along a steep, grassy path, from a rocky rib, with the aid of chains and buckles, we reach a wide gully, that falls from the peaks of Świnica. Traversing the gully requires little effort. Later, the trail leads down the ridge above Świnicki Kocioł (Świnicki Dale) and into Świnicka Przełęcz (Świnicka Pass – 2051 m asl). The pass is deeply serrated between Świnica and Pośrednia Turnia (Middle Crag).

From the pass we turn right and **climb down a steep path, along the black trail**, towards the rocks of the dark Kocioł Świnicki. This is a place, where snow stays till late Spring. The trail traverses the sides of Pośrednia Turnia (Middle Crag) and leads to Stawy Gąsienicowe (Gąsienice Ponds – approx. 45 min) and further to Murowaniec. The blue trail to Karb branches off to the right between Czerwone Stawki (the Red Ponds) and Kurtkowiec. The whole track leads along a rib of Kościelce, which intersects Dolina Gąsienicowa (Gasienice Valley).

The red trail from Świnicka Przełęcz (Świnicka Pass) leads along the path on the Southern, rocky side of Pośrednia Turnia (2128 m asl) and above Walentkowa Dolina (Walentkowa Valley) on the Slovak side. Then it leads up to Skrajna Przełęcz (Extreme Pass – 2071 m asl) and further, all the time along the Southern slopes, onto the Western-most summit of High Tatra – **Skrajna Turnia** (Extreme Crag – 2096 m asl). Unfortunately the trail encircles the peak before reaching Liliowe (Made of Lilies).

We are now on a vast, grassy pass of **Liliowe** at 1952 m asl. The granite Western Tatra end here and the dolomite-calcium rocks of Western Tatra begin. A pleasant **green trail** to Hala Gąsienicowa (Gąsienice Coom – 1 h 15 min) originates on the pass.

*Kasprowy Wierch (1987 m asl): High-ground Meteorological Observatory (upper photo) built on the peak of Kasprowy Wierch.*
*The upper station of cable-railway to Kasprowy Wierch.*
*The picture on the right: the green trail to Kasprowy Wierch through Myślenickie Turnie (Myślenickie Crags).*

From now on the red trail leads along the main ridge of the Western Tatra and reaches the Eastern-most summit of this mountain-chain – **Beskid** (2012 m asl). After making our way through Sucha Przełęcz (Dry Pass – 1950 m asl) we reach **Kasprowy Wierch** (1987 m asl).

# Dolina Bystrej (Bystra Valley)

The vast Dolina Bystrej lays to the South of Zakopane. It stretches along the central part of the Polish Tatra and is easily accessible. One could even say that Dolina Bystrej and the group of Czerwone Wierchy constitute the whole central Polish Tatra. The Northern border of the valley is an elevated region – a Southern closing point of the valleys coming down from Giewont (1894 m asl), Krokwia (1378 m asl) and Kotlina Zakopiańska (940 m asl). The Western side of the valley is created by the ridge ranging from Giewont to Kopa Kondracka (Kondrat Pile – 2005 m asl), through Kondracka Przełęcz (Kondrat Pass – 1725 m asl). In the South the valley is closed by Kondracka Kopa, the peak of which turns to the East, almost at a right angle, Suchy Wierch Kondracki (Dry Kondrat Wierch – 1890 m asl), Suche Czuby (Dry Czuby – 1799 m asl), Gorczykowa Czuba (1913 m asl) and Kasprowy Wierch (1987 m asl).

The Eastern side of Dolina Bystrej consists of the North-eastern ridge of Kasprowy Wierch, Uhrocie Kasprowe (1852 – 1750 m asl), Kopa Magury (Magura Pile – 1704 m asl), Mała Królowa Kopa (Little Queen Pile – 1531 m asl), Wielka Królowa Kopa (Great Queen Pile – 1577 m asl) and further towards the outlet of Skupniów Upłaz valley, Boczań (1208 m asl) and Nosal (1206 m asl – a view at the whole valley).

Dolina Bystrej is narrow in its lower parts and gets wider with altitude. At a certain level, in a post-glacier landscape, seven smaller valleys break off. The most important of them are: Dolina Jaworzynki – located at the lowest altitude, Kasprowa Dolina above it, and the two parallel valleys called Dolina Goryczkowa (Gentian Valley) and Dolina

*Western Tatra with **Goryczkowa Czuba (Gentian Czuba – 1913 m asl)** in the direction of Czerwone Wierchy.*

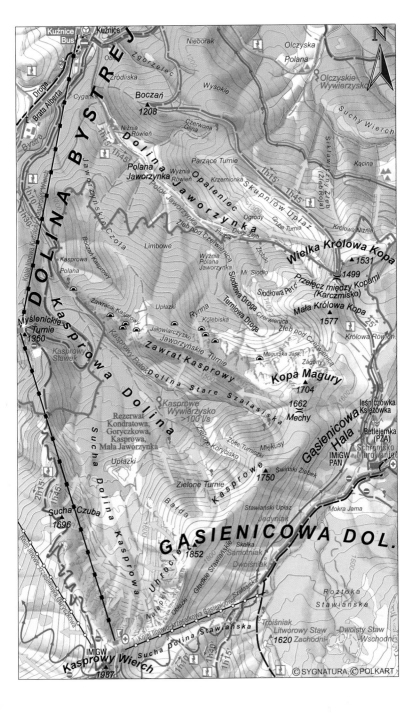

Kuźnice
Bus
Kuźnice
Nieborak
Olczyska
Polana
N
Olczyskie
Wywierzysko
Suchy Wierch
Zgorzelec
Źródliska
Wysokie
Cygarka
Boczań
1208
Czerwona
Glina
Siklawica Żleb
(Żleb Roja)
Kącina
Niżnia
Rówień
Parzące Turnie
Polana
Jaworzynka
Skupniów Upłaz
Wyżnia
Rówień
Krzemionka
Królowa Niżnia
Ogrody
Długi Żleb
Guba Turnia
Wielka Królowa Kopa
▲1531
Limbowe
Żleb pod Czerwienicą
Żlebik
Herbik
1499
Wyżnia
Polana
Jaworzynka
Ml. Siodło
Przełęcz między Kopami
(Karczmisko)
Kasprowa
Polana
Boczań Kasprowy
Siodłowa Droga
Siodłowa Perć
Czerwienica
Mała Królowa Kopa
1577
Myślenickie
Turnie
▲1560
Zawracik Kasprowy
Upłazki
Rynna
Turniowa Droga
Turniowa Droga
Żleb pod Czerwienicą
Królowa Rówień
Kasprowy
Stawek
Jaworzyńskie Turnie
Jałowiarczysko
Kolebiska
Magurska Jask.
Zawrat Kasprowy
Dolina Stare Szałasiska
Zagony
Kopa Magury
▲1704
Kasprowy Potok
Kasprowe
Wywierzysko
>100 l/s
1662
Mechy
Leśniczówka
Księżówka
Rezerwat
Kondratowa,
Goryczkowa,
Kasprowa,
Mała Jaworzynka
Żółte Turniczki
Miękusy
Betlejemka
(PZA)
Upłazki
Żleb Koryciska
IMiGW
PAN
Schronisko
Murowaniec
Sucha Dolina Kasprowa
Zielone Turnie
Świński Żlebek
1750
Sucha Czuba
1696
Bałda
Stawiański Upłaz
Mokra Jama
Jedyniak
GĄSIENICOWA DOL.
Skałka
1852
Samotniak
Dwoiśniak
Roztoka
Stawiańska
Uhrocie
Gładkie Stawiańskie
Szałasiska
Nawrót
Upłazki
Kocioł Goryczkowej
Kocioł Goryczkowej
Kasprowej
Sucha Dolina Stawiańska
Kocioł Gąsienicowa
Trójśniak
Litworowy Staw
1620 Zachodni
Dwoisty Staw
Wschodni
IMiGW
Kasprowy Wierch
▲1987
© SYGNATURA, © POLKART

Kondratowa (Kondrat Valley). Dolina Bystrej is built of sedimentary rocks partially covered by crystalic rocks. After all, we are in the central part of the Polish Tatra – in the region, where the crystalic rock structure meets the sedimentary one.

At the bottom, the valley is covered with forests, while further up, grassy cooms prevail. The grass covers even the ridges, moraines and dales. The post-glacier shape of the valley with the characteristic stream-beds, is perfectly visible during a ride in a cable car.

Three large streams flow along the middle of the valley. These are: Goryczkowy Potok (the Gentian Stream), Kasprowy Potok (the Kasprowy Stream) and Bystra. The last one being an emergency water source for Zakopane.

Goryczkowy Potok originates on Goryczkowa Równia (Gentian Plane – around 1320 m asl) from the junction of two smaller streams. The first, flows down several waterfalls in Dolina pod Zakosy (the Valley of Zigzags), while the second starts in Dolina Świńska (Pigs' Valley). At 1185 m asl, by Myślenickie Turnie, the waters from Gorczykowe Wywierzysko flow into Goryczkowy Potok at the rate of 400 litres/second. This is where the water supply for Kasprowy Wierch comes from. Gorczykowe Wywierzysko is an outlet of a large, krastic, underground stream. Goryczkowy Potok meets Bystra below and to the North of this point.

Kasprowy Potok is propelled by the waters of Kasprowe Wywierzysko (100 litres/second) and Dolina Stare Szałasiska (Old Shacks Valley), that lays at the feet of Kasprowy Zawrat. The stream disappears in the middle part of Dolina Bystrej (Bystra Valley).

Bystra, the main stream of the valley, starts on the side of Kalacka Turnia from Wywierzysko Bystrej (two streams, the upper one at 1175 m asl and the lower one 1165 m asl – 500 l/sec). Goryczkowy Potok converges with Bystra at the level of Kalatówki. Then Kasprowy Potok joins in. The three streams together create a strong current, which flows through Kuźnice into Zakopane.

*High Tatra seen from the ridge of Western Tatra • A cable-car of the cable-railway running over* **Dolina Bystrej (Bystra Valley)** *to the middle station on Myślenickie Turnie (1354 m asl).*

In the middle part of Dolina Bystrej you will find a group of caves. Among them: Jaskinia Goryczkowa (Gentian Cave) and Myślenicka Dziura (Myślenicka Hole) in the slopes of Myślenicka Turnia (Myślenicka Crag), or Jaskinia Bystra (Bystra Cave), Jaskinia Kalacka (Kalacka Cave), Kozi Korytarz (Goats' Corridor) and Dziura za Głazami (The Hole behind Boulders) in the sides of Kalacka Turnia (Kalacka Crag).

Kuźnice (1010 m asl) is the main entrance to Dolina Bystrej. It can be reached from Rondo Kuźnickie in Zakopane by a mini-bus, or by foot, along Aleja Przewodników Tatrzańskich (Tatra Guides' Avenue). You can also take a highlander's carriage or drive with your own car, providing that you first obtained a clearance. The walk can be very interesting, if you decide to go through Polana Kuźnicka (Kuźnicka Glade). On the way, opposite the walls of Nosal, you can find a monument called „Prometeusz Rozstrzelany" („Prometheus shot by the firing squad"). It was made by Władysław Hasior (1928-1999) in 1964, to commemorate the 20 Poles killed here by Germans in 1944.

Around the centre-square of Kuźnice stands a hotel, a tourist house, a restaurant with a cafe, a shop, highlanders' stalls and a parking-lot for buses and carriages. The lower station of the cable railway to Kasprowy Wierch is located above the square, on the threshold of a moraine. During the Winter Kuźnice is flocked by skiers.

**Cable railway to Kasprowy Wierch** consists of two legs. It became operational in 1936, after six months of construction work. Steel cables join the lower station (1028 m asl) in Kuźnice with Myślenickie Turnie (Myślenickie Crags – 1352 m asl). This is the first 2001-metre-long leg. The cable car climbs 324 metres at an average angle of 17,1 degrees. On the right you can see the cloisters by the road to Kalatówki and on Śpiąca Góra (Sleeping Mountain). Further, the bottom of Dolina Kondratowa (Kondrat Valley) and the rib of Długi Giewont (Long Giewont) in the background. The green

*The stony path from Kuźnice to the monasteries of Albertine Sisters and Albertine Brothers and further to Kalatówki.*

Dolina Jaworzynki (Jaworzynka Valley) lays on the left, with two dome-shaped mountains on its ends.

The second leg of the cable railway, from Myślenickie Turnie to Kasprowy Wierch, is 2290 metres long at 28,8 degrees of pitch. The final station along with a restaurant and a cafe is at 1959 m asl. On the second leg, the cable-car climbs 607 metres. The car can take up to 36 passengers and cruises at 18 km/h. It needs 20 min to get from Myślenickie Turnie (Myślenickie Crags) to Kasprowy Wierch. On your left you will see Sucha Dolina Kasprowa (Dry Kasprowa Valley) with the rocky rib of Uhroć Kasprowy. Ski-trails and the ski-lift in Dolina Goryczkowa (Gentian Valley) are on the right.

### Kasprowy Wierch

A 3-hour-long walk from Kuźnice, along the green trail, through Myślenickie Turnie, to Kasprowy Wierch.

The green trail begins at a parking-lot in Kuźnice. Initially it leads along a paved road to Kalatówki, then branches off to the left above the upper station of the cable-railway. One of the main virtues of this track is the fact that it is not frequented by tourists though its tourist values are unprecedented.

We walk along a wide road in the shade of a tall forest. Bystra stream flows alongside. On our way we pass monumental granite boulders. The trail intersects a ski-trail from Dolina Goryczkowa (Gentian Valley) and runs below the cable-railway. It reaches Polana Kasprowa (Kasprowa Glade – 1180-1210 m asl), that lays within terminal and lateral moraines. We are in the lower parts of Dolina Kasprowa. The valley in its upper levels splits into Dolina Stare Szałasiska and Dolina Sucha Kasprowa (Dry Kasprowa Valley). The former reaches the slopes of Uhroć Kasprowy.

*Brother Albert's hermitage* – *the photo on the right.*
*Bottom picture: the monastery of Albertine Brothers on Śpiąca Góra (Sleeping Mountain).*

Within the valley the track climbs a long arc, which leads to calcium-based Myślenickie Turnie (1354 m asl). The crags are carved by precipices on their Western sides. The middle station of the cable-railway lays before us. We are between Dolina Kasprowa and Dolina Goryczkowa (Kasprowa and Gentian Valleys). From here we can see Dolina Kondratowa encircled by the Southern slopes of Giewont. For the remaining part of the excursion we can take the railway, providing there is enough room. Yet walking maybe a better solution, as the most interesting fragments of the trail still lay ahead.

The path from Myślenickie Turnie climbs along a zigzag on the Northern Ridge of Kasprowy Wierch. Calcium rocks gradually disappear from under our feet as we climb higher. They are being replaced by crystalic rocks. This is an grinding effect of two great rock masses, the soft, sedimentary and the hard, crystalic. A wide variety of minerals can be found here, from sundry quartz gneisses and slates to colourful crystals of granites and pegmatites.

In the part just below the summit, the path leads between two lifts – the cable-railway from Myślenickie Turnie and a ski-lift from Równia Doliny Goryczkowej (Gentian Valley Plateau), the upper station of which we pass. One more traverse to the left and we reach the peak of **Kasprowy Wierch**. We walk pass a meteorological observatory, the highest point of which is at 1991 m asl, making the building the highest-located structure in Poland.

We are at almost 1987 m asl, on Kasprowy Wierch – the skiers' mountain.

### Kalatówki
A 30-minute-long walk from Kuźnice, along the blue trail, along monasteries to Kalatówki.

The blue trail begins in Kuźnice by the paved road that exits the parking-lot. The track to Kalatówki is effortless. We quickly reach a snack-bar and a park entrance gate.

*The hostel – Kalatówki hotel.*
*Dolina Kondratowa (Kondrat Valley) with the calcium rib of Długi Giewont (Long Giewont).*
*Polana **Kalatówki** (Kalatówki Glade) with Nosal visible in the distance (the picture on the right).*

The trail leads along a wide road, at a small angle, through a forest.

After approximately 15 minutes we reach the St Albert's nunnery and the hermitage of Brother Albert Adam Chmielowski (1845-1916) – the founder of Zgromadzenie Braci Albertynów Zakonu św. Franciszka Posługujących Ubogim (The Fraternity of Brothers Albertines of the st. Francis Convent of those who Serve the Poor – 1888). Its members are known for their devotion to the issues of the poor and their engagement in the life of Zakopane and the Tatra region. A. Chmielowski along with other monks worked at the construction Zakopane railway, the Oswald Balzer road to Morskie Oko and the black trail to Czarny Staw.

The gate of the cloister is open every day from 6 AM to 7 PM. The place is worth seeing. It was picked by Chmielowski himself and granted to the convent by Władysław Zamoyski. The building blends well with surrounding nature. It is simple and encourages contemplation. The cloister and the chapel were designed by Stanisław Witkiewicz in 1898. Although both structures were made in the Zakopiański Style, they are simple and lack any ornaments. The chapel of Święty Krzyż (Saint Cross) is very similar; it's outfit is humble with a simple ascetic altar. Chatka Pustelnika (Hermit's Hut) was built in the cloister's garden, in 1901. Brother Albert lived here when he visited Zakopane. Currently the hut is a small museum in memory of Adam Chmielowski. In 1902 the hermitage was taken over by Albertine Sisters. The Brothers moved to a larger monastery, or rather a wooden cloister complex. It was built slightly higher, on Śpiąca Góra (Sleeping Mountain – 1186 m asl), in a similar style. The complex can be reached via a short (10 min) pleasant path.

The road goes on. After few minutes it reaches the starting point of the black trail of **Ścieżka nad Reglami (The Path above Prealpes), which leads towards the valleys of Biały** (1 h 20 min) and Strążyska (approx. 2 h). We are on Polana Kalatówka (Kalatówka

*The massif of Giewont seen from the North.*
  *From the left: Długi Giewont (Long Giewont – 1867 m asl), Szczebra (1823 m asl), Giewont (1895 m asl), Żleb Kirkora (Kirkora Gully), Mały Giewont (Little Giewont – 1728 m asl).*

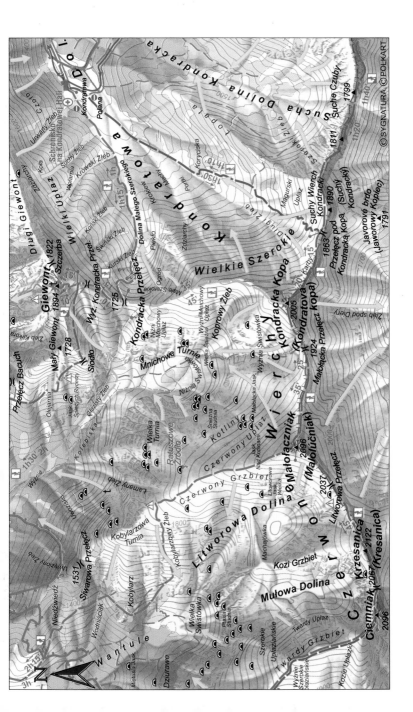

Glade). The structure in front of us is an alpine style hotel-hostel. It was built at 1198 m asl on the highest lateral moraine. It can accommodate up to 86 guests in 1-5-bed rooms. There is also a cafe, a restaurant and two ski-lifts.

**Kalatówki** – a large grassy glade with perfectly preserved lateral moraines, remnants of the glacier from Dolina Bystrej (Bystra Valley). The surroundings of the glade include Kalacki Upłaz (Kalacki Terrace) in the North-west and Kalacka Turnia (Kalacka Crag) with a group of underground caves in the South. In-between you can see Suchy Żleb (Dry Gully). The gully marks a border between Tatra and Kriżański geological regions. Bystra stream, already reinforced by Goryczkowy Potok flows below the Eastern edge of the glade. For a very long time Kalatówki has been a sheep-run. After a short break, it has recently returned to its original function, though in a limited degree.

The mountain visible from Kalatówki, when looking in the direction of the outlet of Dolina Bystrej, is Nosal. The track to Kalatówki and further up, to Hala Kondratowa is a perfect path for pleasant and undemanding walks.

### Through the ridge over Dolina Bystrej (Bystra Valley)

A 3-hour-long walk from Kasprowy Wierch, along the red trail, through Goryczkowa Czuba to Kopa Kondracka, and further along the yellow trail to Kondracka Przełęcz.

After reaching Kasprowy Wierch, the red trail leads below the meteorological observatory and towards the right side of the ridge. Below, to the North, we can see Dolina Kondratowa and Zakopane. On the South side, the vast, Slovak 14-kilometre-long Dolina Cicha Liptowska (Silent Liptowska Valley), the bottom of which marks the border between High and Western Tatra.

*The Western Tatra.* The red ridge-trail to Czerwone Wierchy.

146

The path leads through the rib over Dolina Goryczkowa. The valley is popular among skiers and many ski-trails intersect it. On Wyżnia Równia, you can find a lower station of a 1700-metre-long chair-lift to Kasprowy Wierch, that carries skiers 600 m up.

The path from Kasprowy Wierch to Kopa Kondracka runs through a „crystalic island" among sedimentary rocks of the Western Tatra. The „island" was created by the rocks falling from Giewont's nappe as an effect of great tectonic movements, overlapping of rock masses, which caused some of the older layers to cover the younger ones.

Walking along the rib, we reach Goryczkowa Przełęcz nad Zakosy (1816 m asl). Below, the walls, that carve the ridge at its base, close the post-glacier dale of Dolina pod Zakosy (Valley below Zakosy 1350-1700 m asl). Within few minutes from the pass we reach the grassy Pośredni Wierch Goryczkowy (Middle Gentian Wierch – 1874 m asl). Its shoulder separates Dolina pod Zakosy from the dale of Dolina Świńska (Pig's Valley – 1350-1700 m asl). The trail descends along a steep, grassy slope above the former, onto Goryczkowa Przełęcz Świńska (Gentian Pig's Pass – 1801 m asl). We walk up the main rocky crest of the ridge – Goryczkowa Czuba (1913 m asl). Its Northern ridge, with the imperceptible peak of Kondratowy Wierch, separates Goryczkowa Dolina from Sucha Dolina Kondracka (Dry Kondrat Valley). The trail leads above the former. It traverses the Southern slopes of Suche Czuby (Dry Peaks – 1799 m asl). One should bear in mind that the trail runs through a rib which is carved by very steep precipices on both sides. Thus, taking any shortcuts especially in the direction of Dolina Kondratowa is highly unrecomended.

The trail reaches the Northern side and traverses the slope of Suchy Wierch Kondracki (1890 m asl). Then it leads to Przełęcz pod Kopą Kondracką (1863 m asl). A green trail appears and runs down to the right. It leads through zigzags and steep slopes to the hostel on Hala Kondratowa.

*The hostel on Hala Kondratowa (Kondrat Coom).*

Długi Żleb (Long Gully) falls to the North from the middle of the rib, between Suchy Wierch Kondracki and Kopa Kondracka. Avalanches from this gully can even reach the hostel on Hala Kondratowa. After 20 minutes we reach the first peak of Czerwone Wierchy (Red Wierchy) – **Kondracka Kopa** (2005 m asl). The track continues along the red trail.

On the peak of Kondracka Kopa the ridge turns sharply to the North. A path, marked with yellow colour, leads along it. As it turns away from the peak, the crystalic rocks slowly succumb to calcium rocks from the neighbouring Giewont. Walking along the picturesque rib, we reach Kondracka Przełęcz (1725 m asl – 35 min from Kondracka Kopa).

Two tourist trails intersect on Kondracka Przełęcz. The blue trail leads to Giewont (30 min), or to Hala Kondratowa (1 h), depending on the direction. The yellow trail can lead you to Dolina Małej Łąki (Little Meadow Valley) and Wielka Polana (Great Glade – 1 h 30 min).

**To Giewont through Hala Kondratowa**
A 2-hour-30-minute-long walk from Kalatówki, along the blue trail, through Hala Kondratowa and Przełęcz Kondracka, to Giewont.

The blue trail is a continuation of the track from Kuźnice to Kalatówki. It omits the road from the cloister and leads through the Eastern edge of Polana Kalatówki instead. After leaving the lateral moraine the trail joins the main blue trail on the Southern side of the glade. The path is rocky and leads along a forest-covered side of Kalacka Turnia (Kalacka Crag). Wywierzysko Bystrej (Bystra Underground Outlet) lays nearby, opposite the crag. A track through the forest turns into a wide path and leads towards the outlet of Kondratowa Dolina (Kondrat Valley), along Długi Giewont (Long Giewont). A coom and a hostel on **Hala Kondratowa** (Kondrat Coom) lays ahead.

*The final parts of the blue trail to Giewont. The view of Dolina Kondratowa*

One-lane traffic along the blue trail on Giewont leads to the metal cross (over 17 metres tall) on top. This landmark is very well visible from Zakopane. The idea of placing it here came from the parishioners of Zakopane, and the cross was erected on Giewont in 1901.

The tip of Giewont (1895 m asl).

The hostel lays at 1333 m asl and can accommodate up to 20 guests in multi-bed rooms (6-8). Inside the hostel you will find a snack-bar usually crowded with tourists.

A green trail to Przełęcz pod Kopą Kondracką (Pass below Kondrat Pile – 1 h 30 min) branches off above the hostel. The blue trail leads through the edge of the glade, along the Southern side of Giewont. The path carves into calcium walls and, zigzagging, leads onto Kondracka Przełęcz (1725 m asl). The view onto Dolina Bystrej and the High Tatra widens as we walk. The short rib will lead us onto the calcium rocks of Giewont. On our way we will pass Kondracka Przełęcz Wyżnia (Upper Kondracka Pass), where we are very likely to be joined by the tourists making their way to the summit along the red trail from Dolina Strążyskiej. Unfortunately, during the tourist season this place is undeniably crowded. After all this is **Giewont**, a 1894 m tall mountain that towers above Zakopane.

Giewont falls into Dolina Strążyskiej with a nearly vertical wall, that is well visible from both Kościeliska and Krupówki. From the summit you can marvel at the vast view stretching from Podtatrze and Pasmo Gubałowskie (Gubałówka Belt) through Bielskie and High Tatra Mountains all the way to the vaguely visible tops of Western Tatra.

**Czerwone Wierchy (Red Wierchy)**
A 1-hour-long walk from Kondracka Kopa, along the red trail, through Małołączniak, Krzesanica and Ciemniak.

The red trail, that leads through the ridge of Czerwone Wierchy, begins on Kondracka Kopa (2005 m asl). It is a continuation of the red trail from Kasprowy Wierch. Czerwone Wierchy is the main ridge of Western Tatra.

*The view from Giewont: the ridge above Dolina Gąsienicowa (Gąsienice Valley) with Świnica and Kasprowy Wierch, the ridge above Morskie Oko, Krywań. In the foreground: Goryczkowa Czuba (Gentian Czuba) with the rib leading to Czerwone Wierchy • The path to Giewont • The sign-post on Kondracka Przełęcz (Kondrat Pass).*

The great calcium-based massif of **Giewont** (1895 m asl) stretches from Polana Kalatówki (Kalatówki Glade) along the whole Dolina Kondratowa. Walking from Kalatówki to Giewont along the blue trail on your right you will see (in order of appearance): Długi Giewont (Long Giewont – 1867 m asl) and Szczerba (1823 m asl) – a pass under Giewont. The massif ends on the West with Mały Giewont (Little Giewont – 1728 m asl). The photographs depict the massif as seen from the red trail of Grzybowiecka Dolina. The trail leads further to Dolina Strążyskiej and Zakopane.

The group of **Czerwone Wierchy** consists of four rounded tops: Kondracka Kopa (2005 m asl), Małołączniak (2096 m asl), Krzesanica (2122 m asl) and Ciemniak (2096 m asl). These peaks are separated by wide, shallow passes: Przełęcz pod Kopą Kondracką (Pass below Kondrat Pile – 1863 m asl), Małołącka Przełęcz (Little-meadow Pass – 1924 m asl), Litworowa Przełęcz (Litworowa Pass – 2037 m asl), Przełęcz Mułowa (Mule Pass – 2067 m asl). Czerwone Wierchy rise above Dolina Cicha (Silent Valley), Dolina Kondratowa (Kondrat Valley), Dolina Małej Łąki (Little Meadow Valley), Dolina Miętusia (Miętusia Valley) and Dolina Kościeliska (Kościelisko Valley). Many geological forms can be found here. Mainly dolomites, calcium rocks and granite „crystalic islands", which were shoved onto much younger sedimentary rock layers. The diversification of geological base caused exceptional variety of plant-life. Czerwone Wierchy owe the adjective „red" to a certain plant (called Boletus Bovinus), which grows here in abundance and turns dark red in Autumn, when it blooms. The sedimentary parts of the ridge house numerous caves and underground chambers with long, well developed tunnels. These creations attract speleologists. The sides of the ridge are carved from the North with precipices. Some side ridges also branch off to the North, carrying tourist trails with them. The blue trail, for instance, from Małołącznik leads through Czerwony Grzbiet (Red Rib), above Dolina Litworowa (Litworowa Valley) to Przysłop Miętusi (1189 m asl, 3 h). The red trail leads from Ciemniak, through Twardy Grzbiet (Hard Rib), above Dolina Mułowa (Mule Valley) to Zahradziska (955 m asl, 3 h) and Dolina Kościeliska. Both these trails circumfend a post-glacier dale called **Wielka Świstówka** (Great Świstówka – 1350-1400 m asl). The dale is littered with great calcium boulders, rock thresholds and deep crastic crevasses.

The green trail from Ciemniak leads initially along with the red trail through Twardy Grzbiet. Then near Chuda Przełączka (Slim Pass – 1858 m asl) it branches off due South and reaches Tomanowa Dolina (Tomanowa Valley). The trail leads along the valley to the hostel on Hala Ornak.

*Kopa Kondracka (2005 m asl), Małołącka Przełęcz (Little-meadow Pass – 1924 m asl), Małołącznik (2096 m asl). Other pictures: the path to Ciemniak and further to Dolina Kościeliska.*

# Dolina Kościeliska (Kościelisko Valley)

Dolina Kościeliska lays in the Westrn part of the Polish Tatra mountains. It stretches from Kościelisko to the main ridge of the Western Tatra. The main entrance to the valley is through Kiry, which can be reached from Zakopane by car, or by foot along Droga pod Reglami. In Kiry you will find a parking-lot, a stopping-place for carriages going to Hala Pisana, restaurants with regional cuisine, cafes and an entrance gate to Tatra National Park. The valley itself is one of the most quaint valleys in the whole of Tatra. It can be recommended to anyone, from an experienced mountaineer to a city-slicker with small children.

During our hike along the bottom of Dolina Kościeliska we will be accompanied by Kościeliski Potok (the Kościelisko Stream), which in here is actually called **Kirowa Woda**.

The outlet of Dolina Kościeliska lays between Mały Regiel (Small Bolt – 1142 m asl) with Kończysta Turnia (Kończysta Crag – 1248 m asl) on the East and three forest-covered hills of Kościeliskie Kopki (Kościeliskie Piles: 1113 – 1333 m asl) on the West. A wide track, built in the XIXth century, leads from the outlet of the valley to Hala Pisana. Here it narrows and after passing through few stone bridges it ends by a hostel on Hala Ornak. The track is almost 6 km long and takes 1 h 30 min to walk.

After entering the valley on our right we can see a forester's lodge called „Kościeliska". We reach a narrowing calcium wall, that is being washed by Potok Kościeliski. This is Brama Kantaka (Kantak's Gate) with a plate commemorating this patriot mounted into the rock. The valley widens to create a glade – Wyżnia Kira Miętusia (950 m asl). At this point Potok Kościeliski is nowhere near the trail, it flows through the

*The view of the Western Tatra • Kościelisko Stream*

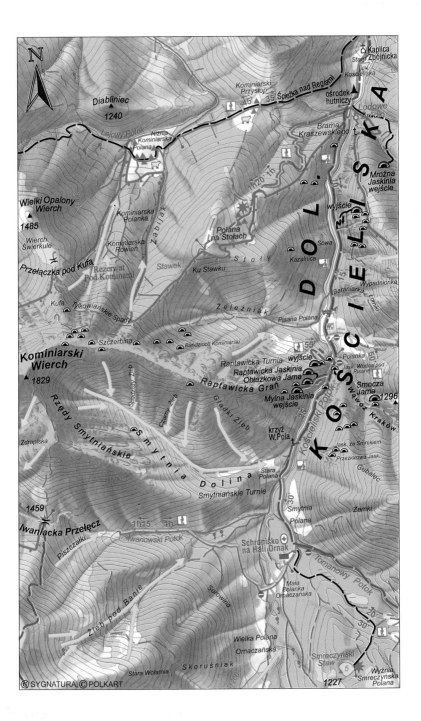

The red trail to Czerwone Wierchy begins on **Zahradziska** glade (955-995 m asl – the exit of Dolina Miętusia) in Dolina Kościeliska.

The path leads through forests and cooms to Polana Upłaz. Then, on the rocky Twardy Upłaz, it joins the green trail from the hostel on Hala Ornak (Ornak Coom), through Dolina Tomanowa.

The photographs depict the path to Ciemniak from Dolina Kościeliska.

forest. There are few sheepherders' shacks on the glade and a highlander's snack-bar. Here you can try a highlander tea, or something more characteristic, like an Oscypek. The glade is used as a sheep-run, while in early Spring it is covered with a carpet of crocuses piercing through the snow.

Walking through a bridge over Potok Kościeliski we enter Cudakowa Polana (Zany Glade). The black trail of Ścieżka nad Reglami (The Path above Prealpes) branches off to the right. It leads through spruce forests above **Dolina Lejowa** (Funnel Valley) to Dolina Chochołowska (Chochołów Valley – approx. 2 h). The black trail leads to the left, to **Dolina Miętusia**. Then along Ścieżka nad Reglami to a long glade called Zahradziska and further through Przysłop Miętusi to Dolina Małej Łąki. A **red trail to Ciemniak** and Czerwone Wierchy (Red Wierchy) branches off from the black trail when the former enters Polana Zahradziska (Zahradziska Glade). The trail is a demanding one, leading through Twardy Upłaz (Hard Terrace), but the effort is worth-making.

Soon we reach **Stare Kościeliska** glade (around 30 min from Kiry). A small shrine, called Zbójnicka Kapliczka (Marauder's Shrine) stands by the edge of the glade. It was built by miners, who mined iron ore in nearby adits. A small ironwork was located here in the XVIIIth century.

The black trail to Jaskinia Mroźna (Frost Cave) branches off to the left in the final part of Stare Kościelisko (Old Kościelisko). The trail leads through a spruce forest along a slope. It takes 20 min to reach the cave. There is a number of caves in the Dolina Kościeliska area. Some of them were made available to tourists. If you are planning to visit such a cave, you should take warmer cloths and a flashlight.

*Zbójnicka Kapliczka (Marauder's Shrine) on Stare Kościeliska glade (970 m asl).*
*In the highlander shack you can try a Bundz (sheep cottage cheese), or an Oscypek... (bottom picture: Wyżnia Kira Miętusia).*

**Jaskinia Mroźna** was discovered in 1934 by Stefan Zwoliński. It was opened for tourists in 1953 and by 1958 was fitted with electric lighting. Jaskinia Mroźna is the most beautiful cave in the Polish Tatra mountains. Any tourist will feel like a speleologist inside it. Prior to entering the cave, you will need to buy a ticket and join a group of other tourists, lead by a guide. The track lays almost **20 metres** below the surface.

The tunnels, in total, are 480 metres long. The entrance is at 1112 m asl, while the exit at 1118 m asl. As you can see the difference of levels is negligible. The cave developed within a long downcast in a calcium rock, in a crevasse widened by travertine waters. Some of the tunnels and chambers of the cave were named, e.g.: Cmentarzysko Nacieków (A Cemetery of Travertines), Wielka Komora (The Great Chamber), Sabałowe Jeziorko (The Pond of Sabała), or Sala Pochyła (Banked Hall). During our tour we will see well developed (crystalic calcium-carbonate) travertines hanging from the ceiling, called stalactites and similar structures, but reaching up from the floor, called stalagmites. Jaskinia Mroźna lays under the massif of Organy (Organs). There are several other caves in the neighbourhood, for example Jaskinia Zimna (Cold Cave).

After leaving Jaskinia Mroźna we walk down a forest track into Dolina Kościeliska. Here we join the typical tourist traffic heading for the hostel on Hala Ornak.

Higher up, the blue trail to **Polana na Stołach** (Glade on The Tables) branches off to the right. It leads along a pebbly path, through a small, red gully (loam slates). The highlanders' shacks on the glade are relics for tourists to see. A short 45-minute-long walk through forests and dolomite formations ends on Suchy Wierch (Dry Wierch – 1428 m asl).

• *Raptawicka Grań (Raptawicka Ridge)– the Eastern, calcium-based shoulder of Kominiarski Wierch (Chimney-sweeper's Wierch) ending with* **Raptawicka Turnia (Raptawicka Crag)** • *Kościeliski Stream flowing through calcium and dolomite gates – Brama Kantaka (Kantak's Gate) shown on the picture.*

One of many distinctive features of Dolina Kościeliska can be found by the outlet of Brama Kraszewskiego (Kraszewski's Gate). It is a duct of an underground stream called **Lodowe Źródło** (the Ice Stream). The water makes way to the surface in a number of strong currents, at the rate of 600 litres/second. Lodowe Źródło is propelled by the waters from under Czerwone Wierchy and flows through a network of underground canals.

The wide track narrows by Brama Kraszewskiego. The rock-gate was named after the great Polish writer to commemorate 50 years of his work. We are slowly approaching **Hala Pisana** (Written Coom). The coom lays between the grassy slopes of Stoły (Tables), Raptawicka Grań (Raptawicka Ridge) and Saturn. This is the final horse-carriage-stop. On the glade you will find wooden tables, benches and a WC.

A track to **Wąwóz Kraków** (Cracow Gorge) branches off to the left above Hala Pisana. The tour around the part of the gorge made available to tourists takes 45 min. The unique formation, carved in calcium rocks, initially makes a sombre impression.

A 37-metre-long cave (without lighting), called **Smocza Jama** (Dragons Lair), is the main tourist attraction here. A long, metal ladder leads to the cave's entrance, as it is located a couple of metres above the bottom of the gorge. The openings leading to Smocza Jama are at 1100 and 1110 m asl. After making a loop, we return to Polana Pisana along the sides of the ridges of Ratusz (Town-hall 1296 m asl) and Saturn (1391 m asl).

An inscription-covered boulder, called **Skała Pisana** (Written Rock – 1020 m asl) can be found to the South of the exit from Wąwóz Kraków, by the main road. A stream, called

*Jaskinia Mroźna (Frost Cave).*
*Crystalic dripstones, stalagmites • The exit of Jaskinia Mroźna • Jaskinia Mroźna (entrance at 1112 m asl, exit at 1118 m asl) – a one-way tunnel, discovered in 1934. It is 480 m long and is fitted with light installation. The photo on the right: Sobałowe Pond.*

Wypływ spod Pisanej (the Efflux from under the Written), flows from under the boulder and through a 250-metre-long tunnel of Jaskinia Pisana (Written Cave) drilled in the calcium rock.

A trail branches off to the right on the opposite side of the road. It is short, but secured with chains, and leads to Jaskinia Raptawicka (Raptawicka Cave), Jaskinia Mylna (Delusive Cave) and Obłazkowa Jama (Obłazkowa Cavern). All these caves are located in the wall of Raptawicka Turnia (Raptawicka Crag). Each takes approximately 1 hour to visit.

**Jaskinia Raptawicka** lays at 1146 m asl, almost 180 metres above the road. A large 10-to-15-metre-high chamber covering 400 m² constitutes the main part of the cave. It can be reached via a ladder. The total length of the cave's tunnels is 140 metres.

**Jaskinia Mylna** (Delusive Cave – entrances at 1098 and 1095 m asl) is a network of partially open passages, which in total are 1300-metres-long. It was created by the waters of a pre-glacier branch of Potok Kościeliski (the Kościelisko Stream – almost 20 metres deep), which carved the calcium rock into its contemporary shape. 300 metres of the passages were made available to tourists. Some of them are wet, slippery and have low ceilings. We should remember to take flashlights and some food with us, as the cave is not called „delusive" for nothing.

**Obłazkowa Jama** is the shortest of the three caves. It lays at 1150 m asl in a slope of the steep Obłazek. 120-metres-long tunnels lead from the entrance chamber. They are wet and have many water dripstones.

The path on the bottom of the valley is surrounded from the West by the sides of Kominiarski Wierch (Chimney-sweeper's Wierch – 1829 m asl), with its Eastern part of

*A short hike through the lower part of the gorge ending in Smocza Jama (Dragon's Lair) – a 37-metre-long cave • The ladder leading to the entrance of Smocza Jama.*

Raptawicka Grań (Raptawicka Ridge) closed by Raptawicka Turnia (Raptawicka Crag). While the slopes of Ciemniak fall from the East.

Once we pass the walls of Raptawicka Turnia, the path narrows. The path crosses a stream via a stone bridge. On our right we can see **Krzyż Pola** (Pol's Cross) of a XIXth century geographer. Dolina Smytnia (Smytnia Valley: 1100 – 1500 m asl) opens behind the cross with Polana Smytnia (Smytnia Glade: 1080 – 1130 m asl). The Northern range of the glacier from Dolina Kościeliska ends here with terminal moraines.

**Kościeliski Potok** (the Kościelisko Stream) begins its flow near the Western edge of Polana Smytnia. It is created by Pyszniański Potok (the Pyszniański Stream), that carries the waters from the whole of Dolina Pyszniańska, and Tomanowy Potok (the Tomanowy Stream) from Dolina Tomanowa.

**The green trail to Tomanowa Dolina** branches off to the left above the Southern edge of Polana Smytnia on a junction of trails. We cross Tomanowy Potok (the Tomanowy Stream) and climb along a path (dolomites and slates) to Tomanowe Polany (Tomanowe Glades). In the past the glades were used as a sheep-run. The green trail turns due North on the Eastern edge of Wyżnia Tomanowa Polana (Upper Tomanowa Glade) and heads towards Chuda Przełączka (1858 m asl), Twardy Grzbiet (Hard Rib) and finally reaches the peak of Ciemniak. The walk from Polana Smytnia (Smytnia Glade) takes approximately 3 hours.

**Tomanowa Przełęcz** (Tomanowa Pass – 1686 m asl) lays above the glades between Ciemniak (2096m asl) and Tomanowy Wierch Polski (Polish Tomanowy Wierch – 1977 m asl). It can be reached from Polana Smytnia in 2 hours. The ridge encircles the upper levels of Dolina Kościeliska (Kościelisko Valley) stretching from its Eastern side to the

*The hostel on Hala Ornak (Ornak Coom) • Pyszniański Stream (picture on the right) after converging with Tomanowy and Iwanowski Streams create Kościelisko Stream (bottom photograph).*

South. This part of the encirclement is completed by the ribs of Tomanowy Wierch, Smreczyński Wierch (2066 m asl), Kamienista (2121 m asl), all the way to Błyszcz (2159 m asl) and Gaborowa Przełęcz (Gaborowa Pass – 1959 m asl). From the West the valley is overlooked by the long ridge of Ornak (1867, 1854 m asl).

The black trail to **Smreczyński Staw** (the Smreczyński Pond) – a strict nature preserve – starts at the junction above the Southern edge of Polana Smytnia. The pond lays at 1227 m asl, between lateral moraines created by the glaciers of Dolina Pyszniańska (Pyszniańska Valley) and Dolina Smreczyńska (Smreczyńska Valley). It is 5,3 m deep, and covers 0,75 ha. The Southern ridge of Dolina Kościeliska reflects in the pond's waters. This is the largest pond in the Polish part of the Western Tatra. We return along the same black trail. The whole walk takes around 30 min.

**Mała Polana Ornaczańska** (Small Ornak Glade) begins near the junction above Polana Smytnia. Schronisko na Hali Ornak (The Hostel on Ornak Coom) stands here, at 1100 m asl. The hostel can accommodate up to 81 persons in 2-4-bed rooms. There is also a snack bar. Since it is the only hostel in the valley and a destination of very many tourists, it tends to be crowded throughout the season.

A yellow trail to Iwaniacka Przełęcz (Iwaniacka Pass) leads above the hostel. It is one of the most significant trails in the valley as it connects Dolina Kościeliska with Dolina Chochołowska.

**Iwaniacka Przełęcz (Iwaniacka Pass)**
A 1-hour-long walk along the yellow trail.

*The Smreczyński Pond (1227 m asl) – 5,3 m deep, covering 0,75 ha. It lays between Tomanowa and Pyszniańska valleys.*

**Dolina Tomanowa (Tomanowa Valley).**

The green trail, that begins by the hostel of Hala Ornak, leads onto the upper level of Dolina Kościeliska – Tomanowa Przełęcz (Tomanowa Pass – 1686 m asl). Dolina Tomanowa (Tomanowa Valley) is encircled by: Smreczyński Żar, Tomanowy Grzbiet (Tomanowy Rib) and Ciemniak (2096 m asl – upper photo).

Further lay the wide Przełęcz Tomanowa (Tomanowa Pass) (bottom picture with Tomanowe Polany visible below the pass), Suchy Wierch (Dry Wierch – 1860 m asl) and Tomanowe Wierchy (1977 m asl).

From the Slovak side you can reach Przełęcz Tomanowa along the red trail leading through Tomanowa Dolina Liptowska.

*Iwaniacka Przełęcz (Iwaniacka Pass – 1459 m asl)* is the simplest connection between the hostel on Hala Ornak (Ornak Coom) and the hostel on Polana Chochołowska (Chochołów Glade – yellow trail).

The pass separates the second rib of Ornak (1854 m asl) from the massif of Kominiarski Wierch (1829 m asl).

This large glade (bottom picture) is a resting-place for many tourists, who often stay here for a longer while surrounded by the summits above Dolina Kościeliska.

The top picture: the path to Przełęcz Iwaniacka from Dolina Kościeliska.

The yellow trail to Iwaniacka Przełęcz begins above the hostel, to the South. The trail crosses Pyszniański Potok (the Pyszniański Stream) through a bridge, then heads due West along the edge of Wielka Polana Ornaczańska and through a tall spruce forest. The path climbs gradually. During the climb we can see the rib above Tomanowa Dolina. The path leads onto Iwaniacka Przełęcz – 1459 m asl. The old trail to Kominiarski Wierch (Chimney-sweeper's Wierch) is closed. The wide saddle of Iwaniacka Przełęcz separates the massif of Kominiarski Wierch from the massif of Ornak, creating a long ridge between Dolina Kościeliska and Dolina Chochołowska.

## Dolina Chochołowska (Chochołów Valley)

Dolina Chochołowska stretches further to the West of the Tatra than any other valley on the Polish side. It can be reached via a road from Zakopane to Witów. Buses and mini-buses carry tourists to Siwa Polana (White Glade) during the season. Here they will find a parking-lot, a bike-rent, highlanders' carriages and an entrance gate to the National Park.

There is a junction one kilometre from the parking-lot. Before we turn left and venture into the heart of Dolina Chochołowska, we should turn right and walk into the forest. Two minutes away lays the point of origin of **Czarny Dunajec**. We are standing in the fork of Kirowa Woda (Kiry Water), that flows from the South-west. A building housing a water measurement station stands on the Northern side of the river.

**Kirowa Woda** becomes Kościeliski Potok in Dolina Kościeliska, while **Siwa Woda** becomes Chochołowski Potok in Dolina Chochołowska.

From the junction we walk along an asphalt road into Dolina Chochołowska. The time needed to walk from the junction to Polana Chochołowska is 2 hours.

On our left, Leśniczówka u Zięby (Zięba's Forester's Lodge), a stylish, highlander hotel with a regional restaurant. A green trail joins the road from the East at **Siwa Polana**.

*Dolina Chochołowska (Chochołów Valley).*
   *The journey from Siwa Polana to the heart of Dolina Chochołowska can be made by a highlander's horse-carriage.*

The trail leads along Droga pod Reglami (The Road below Prealpes) all the way from the ski-jump in Zakopane. Siwa Polana is a flat glade, almost 1 km long and well suited for skiing contests.

The path leads through a forest. Chochołowski Potok flows on our right with Siwiańskie Turnie (Siwiańskie Crags) towering above. Their vertical, dolomite walls are almost 100 m high. The small valleys of Koryciska lay below. Their outlets end by the sides of the stream.

**Polana Huciska** (Huciska Glade) is a former metal-works centre. Iron ore was supplied by adits located in the valleys nearby. We walk pass a dolomite rock standing by the path. It is called Niźnia Brama (Lower Gate). Beside the next narrowing you will find a path branching off to the left. It leads to the outlet of an underground stream, called **Wywierzysko Chochołowskie** (988 m asl), that propels Potok Chochołowski at the rate of 500 l/sec and creates a small pond. The underground stream carries the water from Kominiarski Wierch. Another smaller outlet is on the opposite side of the path.

The black trail of **Ścieżka nad Reglami** begins on the left side of the path. The trail leads along Dolina między Ściany (The Valley between Walls), through forests, to Dolina Kościeliska. This distance takes 2 hours to walk. On the opposite side lays the forest-covered Głębowiec. We approach the rib of Bobrowiec. In the walls of the Western part of the rock-gate lay the hidden tunnels of Szczelina Chochołowska, a long multilayer cave 2300 m long. The uppermost tunnel is 60 m above the lowest one.

We are now almost in the middle of Dolina Chochołowska, between the Eastern ridge of Bobrowiec (1663 m asl) and the Western sides of Kominiarski Wierch. Potok Chochołowski flows along the bottom of the valley. This is the place where the glacier stopped. The rock-laden narrowing is called **Wyżnia Brama Chochołowska** (Upper Chochołów Gate). It acts as the door to the upper part of the valley and its branches. Among them the most significant are: Starorobociańska Dolina (Starorobociańska Valley), Jarząbcza Dolina Chochołowska (Jarząbcza Chochołów Valley) and Wyżnia Dolina Chochołowska (Upper Chochołów Valley).

**Bobrowiec** (1663 m asl) lays on the edge of the ridge encircling Dolina Chochołowska. It also towers above the Slovak Bobrowiecka Dolina (Bobrowiecka Valley) and Juraniowa Dolina (Juraniowa Valley). Turnia Olejarnia (Oil Mill Crag) and Turnia Zawiesista (Viscid Crag) constitute the extension of its rib. Their 150 m high precipices limit Wyżnia Brama Chochołowska. Their walls are made of layers of sandstone, that range from the Gate to the Western slopes of Kominiarski Wierch. Przełęcz Bobrowiecka (Bobrowiecka Pass – 1356 m asl) separates Bobrowiec from Grześ (Gregory). The pass is a convenient connection between Polana Chochołowska (Chochołów Glade) and Bobrowiecka Dolina (Bobrowiecka Valley). The green trail leads from the former to the peak of Bobrowiec and further through Juraniowa Przełęcz (Juraniowa Pass) to the Slovak side. From the dwarf-mountain-pine-covered Bobrowiec you can see the whole Dolina Chochołowska.

**Kominiarski Wierch** (1829 m asl) is a vast massif, that rises above Dolina Kościeliska and Dolina Chochołowska. The peak is made of white calcium-rocks and dolomites. Raptawicka Grań (Raptawicka Ridge) stretches from the summit towards Dolina Kościeliska, while on the other side grassy slopes reach Dolina Chochołowska. On the

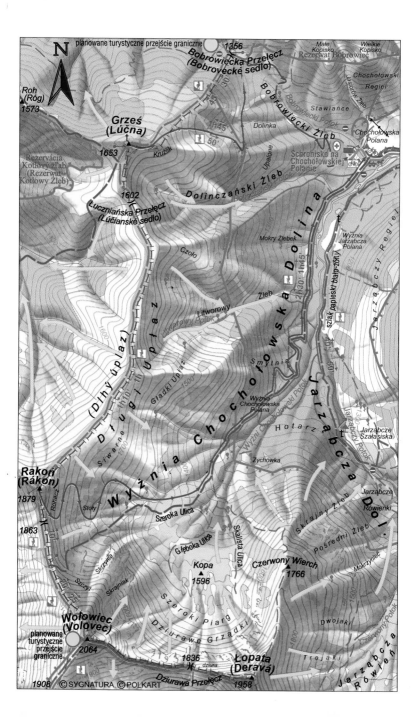

North, the slopes of Tylkowe Kominy (Tylkowe Chimneys) reach Dolina Lejowa (Funnel Valley). On the South the sides of Kominiarski Wierch meet another long ridge, Ornak, via Iwaniacka Przełęcz. Kominiarski Wierch houses a couple of caves. Among them: Lejowa Szczelina (Funnel Orifice), Bańdzioch Kominiarski, Troista. There are also open caves. Currently Kominiarski Wierch is closed for tourists. Too bad....

After walking through Wyżnia Brama Chochołowska (Upper Chochołów Gate) we pass a forester's lodge and reach a junction of streams. Here, at 1040 m asl, Starorobociański Potok (the Starorobociański Stream) meets Potok Chochołowski (the Chochołów Stream). The yellow trail to Iwaniacka Przełęcz (Iwaniacka Pass – 1,5 h) begins on our left together with the black trail leading to Dolina Starorobociańska (to Siwa Przełęcz – under 3 h).

After few minutes of walking along the path we reach Polana Trzydniówka (Three-day Glade). The red trail to Trzydniowiański Wierch (Three-day Wierch – above 2 hours) begins here. After leaving the glade we walk through a bridge and onto Polana Chochołowska (Chochołów Glade).

**Polana Chochołowska**, the heart of Dolina Chochołowska, lays at 1090-1160 m asl at the foot of Bobrowiec. The mountain is very distinctive due to the white peaks of Mnichy Chochołowskie rising from it. The ridge above the glade is created by: Grześ (1653 m asl), Długi Upłaz (Long Terrace), Rakoń (1879 m asl), Wołowiec (2064 m asl), Łopata (the Shovel – 1958 m asl), Jarząbczy Wierch (2137 m asl), Kończysty Wierch (2002 m asl), Trzydniowiański Wierch (Three-day Wierch – 1758 m asl), Mały Kopieniec (Small Mound – 1257 m asl) and Wielki Kopieniec (Great Mound –1329 m asl). A couple of highlanders sell raw and smoked sheep-cheese from shacks standing by the path. Some shepherding still takes place here. The glade gets covered with crocuses in the final days of Winter.

*Siwiańskie Turnie (Siwiańskie Crags – 1065 m asl) – a group of dolomite crags, that fall with 100-metre-tall walls down to the Chochołów Stream • The Chochołów Stream • Taking the sheep to mountain pastures in Autumn.*

A charming little wooden chapel of John the Baptist stands on the edge of the glade, below Mnichy Chochołowskie (Chochołów Monks). People who visit this area often make a short stop at the chapel for a moment of contemplation.

Schronisko na Polanie Chochołowskiej (The Hostel on Chochołów Glade) stands at 1148 m asl, on the edge of the glade. It can accommodate up to 133 tourists in 3-5-bed rooms. It also has large dining room, and a terrace, where one also can eat a meal.

In June 1983 the hostel was visited by the Pope Jan Paweł II.

**Wołowiec**
A 3-hour-long walk from the hostel, along the yellow trail, through Grześ, Długi Upłaz, Rakoń to Wołowiec.

The yellow trail to Grześ (Gregory) leads along an old mining road of Bobrowiecki Żleb (Bobrowiec Gully) towards Bobrowiecka Przełęcz (Bobrowiec Pass). Bobrowiecki Potok (the Bobrowiec Stream) flows along the trail. Under the pass the path turns sharply to the left, it traverses the slope and leads onto the summit of Grześ (1653 m asl with a cross on top). The mountain is made of a layer of quartzite sandstone, that lays on a crystalic bed. The yellow trail joins the blue trail, that leads from Slovak Dolina Jamnicka (Jamnicka Valley) through Wołowiec and Bobrowiecka Przełęcz to Bobrowiecka Dolina. The time needed to reach Grześ from the hostel is 1 h 45 min.

The blue trail leads through the crystalic rocks of Długi Upłaz (Long Terrace), above the dale of Wyżnia Dolina Chochołowska (Upper Chochołów Valley). The ridge of Trzydniowiański Wierch (Three-day Wierch) and Ornak can be seen from the rib. After an hour we reach Rakoń (1879 m asl) and later Wołowiec. Below, on our right, we can see

*St. John Baptist's Chapel on Polana Chochołowska (Chochołów Glade)* • *Shepherding on Polana Chochołowska. The massif of Kominiarski Wierch (1829 m asl) in the background.*

Rohacka Dolina (Rohacka Valley) with the well visible nature preserve of Rohackie Stawy (the Rohackie Ponds).

The blue trail is joined by the green trail in the middle of the rib between Rakoń and Wołowiec. This trail leads from the hostel, along **Wyżnia Dolina Chochołowska** (Upper Chochołów Valley) and its post-glacier dale (with moraines). Wyżni Potok Chochołowski (the Upper Chochołów Stream) originates in this dale. The stream creates the main current of **Chochołowski Potok** after converging with Jarząbczy Potok (the Jarząbczy Stream). 2 h 30 min are needed to reach the saddle on the rib from the hostel.

Wołowiec (2064 m asl) is an international summit. Three ridges meet here. One from Kończysty Wierch in the East, another from the sharp granite peaks of Rohacze in the South-east, and finally one from Bobrowiecka Przełęcz in the North. The blue trail from Jamnicka Dolina leads through Wołowiec, then along its Northern ridge to Bobrowiecka Dolina (Bobrowiecka Valley).

### Wołowiec – Kończysty Wierch

A 2-hour-30-minute-long walk from Wołowiec along the red trail, through Łopata (the Shovel), Jarząbczy Wierch to Kończysty Wierch.

The rib from Rakoń changes its heading on Wołowiec and leads due East. The path leads through a ridge above the dales of two upper branches of Dolina Chochołowska (Chochołów Valley), Wyżnia Dolina Chochołowska (Upper Chochołów Valley) and Dolina Jarząbcza (Jarząbcza Valley). Their tall sides, usually covered with grass, are carved by short precipices in few places, especially in the upper parts.

*Mnichy Chochołowskie (Chochłów Monks – 1500 m asl) – dolomite crags on the slopes of Bobrowiec (1663 m asl) towering above Polana Chochołowska.*

A path from the peak of Wołowiec leads due East to Dziurawa Przełęcz (The Pass with holes – 1836 m asl) above Jamnickie Stawy (the Jamnickie Ponds) of Jamnicka Dolina (Jamnicka Valley – blue trail from Wołowiec). Further, it climbs onto the wide peak of Łopata (the Shovel – 1958 m asl) and circumfends it along the Slovak side of the mountain. The North-bound ridge of Łopata ends with Czerwony Wierch (Red Wierch – 1766 m asl) and towers above Jarząbcza Równia (Jarząbcza Plane). On the short leg from Niska Przełęcz (Short Pass – 1831 m asl) to Jarząbczy Wierch (2137 m asl) we will climb 300 metres traversing and zigzagging through rocks. We are now above three valleys: Jarząbcza, Jamnicka and Raczkowa. The rib heading to the Slovak side leads (green trail) to Raczkowa Czuba (2193 m asl). It is the second highest summit in Western Tatra Mountains.

After 30 min of walking from Jarząbczy Wierch we reach Kończysty Wierch (2002 m asl). The red trail leads further towards Błyszcz and Pyszniańska Przełęcz (Pyszniańska Pass). The green trail to Trzydniowiański Wierch (Three-day Wierch – 45 min) leads down.

**Trzydniowiański Wierch (Three-day Wierch)**
A 3-hour-30-minute-long walk from Polana Trzydniówka (Three-day Glade), along the red trail, to Trzydniowiański Wierch and Dolina Jarząbcza.

The red trail begins just below Polana Chochołowska (Chochołów Glade) on Polana Trzydniówka (Three-day Glade) at the foot of Wielki Kopieniec (Great Kopieniec – 1257 m asl). It heads South, climbing a steep slope of Krowi Żleb (Cow's Gully), then along the sides of Wielki and Mały Kopieniec (Great and Little Kopieniec). In the upper part of the climbout the path leads through 2-metre-high dwarf-mountain-pines. It is a relatively rare sight. Below, on the right, we can see Polana Chochołowska and Bobroweic. We walk down

*The hostel on Polana Chochołowska • Kominiarski Wierch seen from the path to the hostel.*

NA TO MIEJSCE PRZYBYŁ
PAPIEŻ JAN PAWEŁ II
W DNIU 23 CZERWCA 1983 R.

"MOGŁEM W DNIU DZISIEJSZYM
SPOJRZEĆ Z BLISKA NA TATRY
I ODETCHNĄĆ POWIETRZEM
MOJEJ MŁODOŚCI."

/JAN PAWEŁ II/

the wide, grass-covered Grań Kulawca (Kulawiec Ridge) above Trzydniowiańska Dolina (Three-day Valley) and reach Trzydniowiański Wierch (Three-day Wierch – 1758 m asl). The hike from Trzydniówka to the peak takes approximately 2 h 15 min.

The red trail descends with wide zigzags down a post-glacier dale, to **Dolina Jarząbcza** (Jarząbcza Valley), one of the main branches of Dolina Chochołowska (Chochołów Valley). After entering the forest and crossing Jarząbczy Potok (the Jarząbczy Stream) you will find the place (marked by a plaque), where the Pope rested during his excursion through Dolina Jarząbcza. Further on, the path leads through forest clearings to Polana Chochołowska. The distance from Trzydniowiański Wierch (Three-day Wierch) to the glade takes 1 hour to walk.

**Trzydniowiański Wierch – Kończysty Wierch**
A 1-hour-long walk along the green trail.

The trail leads along the ridge above Dolina Jarząbcza (Jarząbcza Valley) and Starorobociańska Dolina (Starorobociańska Valley), and traverses the slopes of Czubik. It is a fully open terrain. Below, to the East lay Dudowe Stawki (Dudowe Ponds: 1675 – 1690 m asl) – a group of small ponds on the upper level of Starorobociańska Dolina.

**Dolina Starorobociańska (Starorobociańska Valley)**
A 2-hour-45-minute-long walk along the black trail to Siwa Przełęcz (White Pass).

The black trail begins above Wyżnia Dolina Chochołowska (Upper Chochołów Valley) and heads South, into the forest, along Starorobociański Potok (the

*Kończysty Wierch (2002 m asl) reached after walking along the green trail, through the ridge from Trzydniowiański Wierch (Three-day Wierch) to the country's border • The red trail from Polana Trzydniówki (Three-day Glade) to Trzydniowiański Wierch (1758 m asl) leads among 2-metre-tall dwarf-mountain-pines.*

**Starorobociański Wierch (2176 m asl)** is the highest summit of the Polish Western Tatra mountains. Its granite pyramid towers above Starorobociańska Dolina on the Polish side and Raczkowa Dolina on the Slovak side.

The peak lays in the main ridge of the Western Tatra between Kończysty Wierch (2002 m asl) and Błyszcz (2159 m asl).

The post-glacier dale in the upper part of Starorobociańska Dolina carves the slopes of Starorobociański Wierch.

Starorobociański Wierch (2176 m asl)

Taking a rest on Trzydniowiański Wierch

The red ridge-trail to Trzydniowiańki Wierch (1758 m asl)

Starorobociański Stream). A yellow trail keeps it company all the way to the edge of Polana Iwanówka (Iwanówka Glade), where the trails split.

The path leads along the bottom of the valley between the rib of Ornak and Trzydniowiański Wierch (Three-day Wierch). In the past this was a copper mining region. On the sides you can see lateral moraines, remnants of the glacier. The path reaches Starorobociańska Równia (Starorobociańska Plane – 1330-1390 m asl) South from Starorobociański Wierch. We climb up Żleb pod Pyszną (The Gully below Pyszna). In its middle we turn and head South for Siwa Przełęcz (White Pass). On the opposite slope, Dudowe Stawki (Dudowe Ponds) and grass-covered terraces of **Cielęce Tańce** (Calf's Dance: 1600-1700 m asl). You can almost hear the sounds of the calfs which once romped here.

A green trail leads from Siwa Przełęcz (White Pass) to Gaborowa Przełęcz (Gaborowa Pass – 1959 m asl) and the main ridge of Western Tatra. Starorobociański Wierch lays in the West, while Błyszcz is in the East.

### Kończysty Wierch – Błyszcz
A 2-hour-long walk from Kończysty Wierch, along the red trail, through Starorobociański Wierch, Gaborowa Przełęcz, to Błyszcz.

The trail is a continuation of the red trail leading along the ridge above Dolina Chochołowska (Chochołów Valley), from Wołowiec to Kończysty Wierch. We begin this hike on Kończysty Wierch (2002 m asl). In the South we can see Raczkowa Dolina (Raczkowa Valley) along with a couple of ponds. A yellow trail leads from there and joins the ridge on Przełęcz Starorobociańska (Starorobociańska Pass – 1975 m asl). We struggle

*The ridge of Ornak. Starorobociański Wierch and the main ridge of Western Tatra visible in the background • Siwe Stawki (White Ponds – 1716 m asl, 1718 m asl) in Pyszniańska Dolina • A sign-post on Siwa Przełęcz (White Pass – 1812 m asl). It shows the way to Raczkowa Przełęcz (1959 m asl) or to Ornak in the direction of Kominiarski Wierch (Chimney-sweeper's Wierch). The black trail from Siwa Przełęcz leads along Starorobociańska Dolina to the track in Dolina Chochołowska (Chochołów Valley).*

up the highest summit of Polish Western Tatra – **Starorobociański Wierch**. The mountain shaped like a pyramid towers above its surroundings. We are at 2176 m asl. The ridge leads East onto a carved Gaborowa Przełęcz (Gaborowa Pass). We move on along the red trail and after few minor eminences we reach Błyszcz (2159 m asl). The mountain constitutes the end of this rib, which begun on the Slovak mountain of Bystra (2248 m asl).

From Błyszcz, the red trail leads along the ridge and after 1 h reaches Pysznianska Przełęcz (Pysznianska Pass – 1788 m asl). We return the same way.

## Ornak through Iwaniacka Przełęcz (Iwaniacka Pass)
A 4-hour-long walk from Iwanówka, along the yellow and the green trails, through Iwaniacka Przełęcz, Ornak, Siwa (White) and Gaborowa Przełęcz (Gaborowa Pass).

The yellow trail to Iwaniacka Przełęcz (Iwaniacka Pass) begins above Wyżnia Brama Chochołowska (Upper Chochołów Gate). It leads through a forest, along the sides and the bottom of Iwaniacka Dolina (Iwaniacka Valley). It is the most convenient connection between Dolina Chochołowska (Chochołów Valley) and Dolina Kościeliska (Kościeliska Valley). Within 1 h 30 min we reach a wide meadow on a pass, a perfect resting place for many tourists.

The green trail to Ornak begins by a sign-post and leads into a forest and further among dwarf-mountain-pines. We zigzag up, above the pass. The Southern side of Kominiarski Wierch, with the protruding crags and rock-pikes, becomes more visible. The ridge of Ornak is grassy and clear of trees, hence the sights can be breathtaking. It leads above Starorobociańska Dolina (Starorobociańska Valley) and Dolina Pysznianska (Pysznianska Valley).

The ridge rises in few places and creates the main peaks: Suchy Wierch Ornaczański (Dry Ornak Wierch – 1832 m asl), Pośredni Ornak (Middle Ornak – 1854 m asl) and the

*Ornak (1854 m asl) separates Starorobociańska Dolina from Pysznianska Dolina. The mountain is in turn fenced off from Kominiarski Wierch (1829 m asl) by Iwaniacka Przełęcz (Iwaniacka Pass – 1459 m asl). The green ridge-trail • Dudowy Stawek (the Dudowy Pond) in Starorobociańska Dolina.*

**Raczkowe Stawy (Raczkowe Ponds) – Slovak side.**

The border-trail from Błyszcz, through Starorobociański Wierch, Kończysty Wierch, Jarząbczy Wierch and the ridge of Raczkowa Czuba (2193 m asl, the second tallest summit of Western Tatra after Bystra • 2248 m asl) encircling Raczkowa Dolina (Raczkowa Valley). A group of ponds lay in the bottom of Zadnia Raczkowa Dolina (Rear Raczkowa Valley). These ponds are called: Suchy (Dry), Skrajny (Extreme) and Zadni (Rear). Late into the Summer they create a single lake.

The pictures depict Raczkowe Stawy and Jarząbczy Wierch (2137 m asl)with the ridge to Raczkowa Czuba.

The yellow trail from the pass below Kończysty Wierch leads to Slovak Republic.

**The Western Tatra** seen from Orna-czańska Przełęcz (bottom photograph) and from Trzydniowiański Wierch (upper photo). The pictures depict: Łopata (the Shovel –1958 m asl) and Wołowiec (2064 m asl) with the side-ridge to Rakoń and Grześ (Gregory).

On the left side of both the pictures you can see Raczkowa Czuba (2193 m asl) and Jarząbczy Wierch (2137 m asl).

Slovak Rohacze lay in the background. In the foreground of the bottom picture you can see the ridge of Trzydniowiański Wierch with Czubik (1846 m asl).

tallest of the three – rocky Zadni Ornak (Rear Ornak – 1867 m asl). The former is connected to a separate group of elevations called Siwe Skały (White Rocks) in their upper level.

After making its way through the last groups of rocks the path descends. Little ponds of Siwe Stawki (White Ponds: 1716, 1718 m asl) lay to the left, in Pyszniańska Dolina (Pyszniańska Valley). The trail reaches Siwa Przełęcz (White Pass). More than 2 hours are required to walk through the ridge of Ornak.

### Post scriptum

A couple of young people embracing on the summit of Kończysty Wierch end this guidebook. They are full of confidence that they will return, just like the memories of every mountain excursion they made. Nostalgia.

We hope that, when you will be back home, our book will bring back the memories of your stay in the Tatra mountains, both the beautiful, sunny ones and the less pleasant of rain and frost. This was the main idea behind the publication. We tried to underline the general character of the Polish Tatra, their uniqueness, and attempt to answer the question: why do Tatra mountains have such a paramount influence on every single generation of Poles?

Each and every one of us takes their own path.

# Index of geographical names
A list of significant geographical names that appear in the text.

**Tourist Information**

**Zakopane**

Tatrzańskie Ochotnicze Pogotowie Ratunkowe
(Tatra Volunteer Rescue Unit) – ul. Piłsudskiego 63a – tel. 634-44
Policja (Police) – ul. Jagielońska 32 – tel. 997
Straż Pożarna (Fire Brigade) – ul. Orkana 2a – tel 998
Pogotowie Ratunkowe (Ambulance Service) – ul. Kamieniec 10 – tel. 999
Pomoc drogowa (AAA) – tel. 981, 96-37, 704-20

Centrum Informacji Turystycznej
(Tourist Information Centre) – ul. Kościuszki 17 – tel.122-11
Tatrzański Park Narodowy
(Tatra National Park Administration) – Rondo Kuźnickie – tel. 637-99
Przedsprzedaż biletów kolejowych
(Railroad tickets reservation) – ul. Chramcówki 35 – tel. 150-31
Informacja telefoniczna PKP
(Railroad Information) – tel. 145-04, PKS (Bus Information) – tel. 146-03
Informacja meteorologiczna
(Meteorological Information) – ul. Sienkiewicza 26c – tel. 630-19

Szpital (The Hospital) – ul. Kamieniec 10 – tel. 120-21
Przychodnia Rejonowa (Regional Policlinic) – ul. Gimnazjalna 8 – tel. 688-44

Hostels:
Nad Morskim Okiem – tel. 776-09
Dolina Pięciu Stawów – tel. 776-07
Dolina Roztoki – tel. 774-42
Hala Gąsienicowa – tel. 126-33
Kalatówki – tel. 636-44
Hala Kondratowa – tel. 152-14
Hala Ornak – tel. 705-20
Polana Chochołowska – tel. 705-10
Schronisko Młodzieżowe (Youth Hostel) – tel. 662-03
Camping „Pod Krokwią" – tel 122-56

Muzeum Tatrzańskie (Tatra Museum) – ul Krupówki 10 – tel. 152-05
Muzeum Stylu Zakopiańskiego w „Kolibie" (The Muzeum of Tatra Style in „Koliba") –
ul. Kościeliska 18 – tel. 136-02

Up-to-date information regarding addresses, prices, opening hours of museums,
galleries, cinemas, theatres, planned festivities in Zakopane and Podhale can be found
in the regional Tygodnik Podhalański.

**A list of photographs not described in the text, according to page numbers:**

**A list of maps:**